Marriage Maintenance 3K

SAVING YOUR MARRIAGE FROM BREAKDOWNS

SCOTT M. CADORETTE, CARLA D. CADORETTE

Contents

Foreword

Our Marriage Beliefs

"Love is patient, love is kind. It does not envy, it does not boast, it is not proud. It is not rude, it is not self-seeking, it is not easily angered, it keeps no record of wrongs. Love does not delight in evil but rejoices with the truth." 1 Corinthians 13:4-6 NIV

Marriage is a covenant relationship designed by God for the joining of one man and one woman into one flesh, not to be undone by any human action, as scripture describes in Matthew 19:4-6:

> "Haven't you read," he replied, "that at the beginning the creator 'made them male and female,' and said, 'For this reason a man will leave his father and mother and be united to his wife, and the two will become one flesh'?"

The marriage covenant mirrors the relationship that God has established with His people.

- God should be in a place of sovereignty over all marriages.

- Marriage is in constant need of God's guidance, grace, and mercy.

- Marriage is other-centered and not for self-serving purposes.

- Marriage is a foundation upon which to build a family.

Rationale

The marriage covenant as designed by the Creator is under constant assault from the evil plans of Satan and the misdirected ideals of this world. For this reason, couples should be prepared by:

- Developing a thorough understanding of the sanctity of marriage according to biblical principles

- Learning how to commit to a life-long marriage in serving the Lord and one another

- Employing safeguards to deal with the relentless attacks upon their marriage union

- Working together to raise children in a Christ-centered home

Jeremiah 6:14 says, "They dress the wound of my people as though it were not serious. 'Peace, peace,' they say, when there is no peace." Church leaders up until now have behaved as if the heartache from marital struggles, past trauma, and broken marriages is not serious, but it is very serious. It needs to be tended as a serious injury with the need for treatment and rehabilitation. That is the purpose of this study.

Prologue

I hope you are one of those people who reads the prologue in the front of books. Funny. If you already read that sentence then you *are* a prologue reader, or *at least* you are reading your first one. If you are a first-timer, don't feel bad because I always skipped them too. Then one time I decided to read one. Originally I skipped it, but I thought the book was so good that I wanted to read more, and the only thing left while waiting on the next book was the prologue. So, I went back to the front of the book and read my first prologue. That prologue was written just as well as the book, but what I learned that day is that the prologue is not giving you a preview of what you are about to read; it is essentially *preparing* you for the read.

Maybe you consider yourself broken, or maybe you consider your marriage broken, or maybe both. This book is for **you** because we know the Mechanic that can fix broken things. Maybe you believe you have it all together and your marriage is doing just fine. This book is for **you** because we know you do not want a marriage that is *just fine*. Maybe your marriage is great, and you and your spouse are doing so much better than when you were first married. This book is for **you** because you need to maintain that high level of excellence. Maybe you are about to take the plunge and get married. This book is for **you** because if you are calling marriage *taking the plunge*, then you will need to figure out how to swim … FAST!

Spoiler alert! This book was not written by perfect people! That's right. This book was written by broken people. Shhh! Have you heard the song "Broken Things," by Matthew West? In the song he sings the words "But if it's true You use broken things, then here I am Lord, I'm all Yours." That is not unlike the call I received from the Lord in the winter of 2021. I have personally failed in multiple marriages and Carla has failed in a previous marriage as well, yet the Lord tapped me on the shoulder and said He has a big job for the two of us. He said, "I am going to have you and Carla start a marriage ministry that is going to have a profound impact on marriages around the world."

The normal excuses I would have given would be: I am just too old, I have failed more often than not in marriage, I do not have the advanced training and degrees, I live in a small town, I do not have the financial resources necessary, I do not have the time, I am an introvert, and I have lots of anxiety. I am sure there are more I could have come up with on top of those. But instead, I was filled with confidence to say, "Here I am Lord, I'm all Yours." I also did not suddenly wonder what I just did. Instead, I immediately told Carla what we were going to be doing for the rest of our time here in this life.

Here is one more interesting back-story regarding our ministry: as part of this calling, Carla and I started pursuing our Doctor of Education degrees. Our plan was to wait until we finished our degrees to start our ministry and this book. Shortly after we started working on our respective programs at Liberty University, I felt as if God was nudging me to talk to our pastor, Duane, about our desire to start a ministry now. I conferred with Carla and she said we should be patient and stick to the plan, and I agreed. Then God spoke to me again, asking why I was listening to Carla instead of Him; He added that our education will be a resource, but not The Source. After meeting with Pastor Duane, our couples ministry project was underway.

I know many of you may be feeling some anxiety about your current situation, wondering if this book is going to help you and your marriage. I would feel the same way about writing this book if I did not know in my heart that this is what God wanted Carla and me to do. If you are still reading our prologue at this point, I can assure you that God Himself has connected you with this book and this ministry.

As you read this book, you will find that some things are powerful to you: lightbulb moments that change your perceptions. And you'll find things that don't do anything for either of you. Everyone is different. Try everything at least a few times, a few days, a couple of weeks, and if you both feel something is not relevant to you, let it go. But give everything a chance and some commitment. Even if it doesn't apply to you, it may mean the world to your spouse or to other couples you meet. Sometimes the tiniest thing can make a world of difference to someone.

Please pray this prayer with us before you start ...

Heavenly Father,
You have created this wonderful covenant of marriage, a beautiful vessel for one man and one woman to share their lives as one. Father God, we thank You for this blessing of sharing our lives together in service to You. We surrender this marriage to Your sovereignty and ask for Your continual guidance in defending this marriage against all sinful attacks of the evil one and this world. Lord, please fill our hearts with Your love for one another, and strengthen this marital bond to glorify You. Please show us Your grace and grant us forgiveness for our shortcomings in not fully respecting this union the way You intended. As we embark upon this journey, open our hearts and minds to listen to the message You intend for us to hear. Gracious Father, we now lift this marriage up to You to mold it as You desire into a marriage that will honor You, fill our lives with joy, and equip us to deliver hope to other marriages.
In the Holy Name of Jesus, we pray. Amen

My Agreement

I _____ understand that *Marriage Maintenance 3000* is a course designed to help couples strengthen their marriage relationships. As such, individuals and couples may openly discuss information of a personal nature to help improve their own marriage as well as other marriages. As a participant in this class, I understand that I have certain moral responsibilities to the members and leaders of this group, and they have the same moral responsibilities to me. With this understanding, I commit to holding this sensitive information in the strictest confidence and will not discuss it with anyone other than the person who disclosed this information without their consent.

Next, I accept that there are certain expectations required of me as part of this group, and I commit to the group to do the following:

- Be positive, affirming, encouraging, and attentive.

- Be trustworthy, respectful, and non-judge-mental.

- Be patient, kind, and receptive.

In addition to my responsibilities to the group, I also commit to the following responsibilities to my spouse and our marriage:

- Put time into the preparation activities.

- Actively listen and participate.

- Be honest and open in communication.

- Respond with love, kindness, and humility.

Finally, I acknowledge this class is only one helpful tool for maintaining a healthy marriage, and I must commit to consistently working on my contribution to our marriage. I recognize that I can go to God anytime in prayer, I can speak kindly with my spouse, I can find a mentor couple we can learn from, and my facilitators are willing to help. I commit to giving 100% effort to strengthen, preserve, and maintain a healthy marriage; a great marriage is not 50-50, it needs to be 100-100.

Signed _____

Date _____

Chapter 1

THIS IS MARRIAGE

1.0 Preparing Your Heart

"That is why a man leaves his father and mother and is united to his wife, and they become one flesh. Genesis 2:24

Objective: This week we will identify the differences between the world's view of marriage and God's plan for marriage.

Before coming to class each week, take the time to read this section at the beginning of each chapter. The purpose is to prepare your heart and mind for the topic of the week and give you an idea of what will be discussed. During class, you will complete the "Group Session" section. Then, during the week, you'll complete the "On Your Own" section. After you and your spouse have completed your individual homework, come together and do the "Couple Time" section. We recommend you get your homework done early in the week so that you have time to *think about* the topic of the week before jumping into the next topic. This will also give you a greater opportunity to *apply* what you learn prior to the next class. Now let's get started!

1.1 Group Session

"That is why a man leaves his father and mother and is united to his wife, and they become one flesh. Genesis 2:24

Are you a statistics fan? Lots of people aren't. I mean, 99% of the statistics people state are made up anyway. Just kidding, I made that up. But there is definitely some value in learning some numbers someone else analyzed. My eyes start to cross when I try to analyze a bunch of research myself, but thankfully we have Scott who loves this stuff, and here are some real and relevant statistics.

Marriage by the Numbers

- _____ of all Americans over the age of ___ are married.

- The median marriage age for men is _____ and _____ for women.

- _____ out of every _____ marriages is a remarriage.

- _____ Americans are cohabitating with

a partner.

- The marriage rate in the US is _____ per 1000 people while the divorce rate is _____ per 1000 people.

- ____% of marriages are first marriages, ____% have one spouse remarried, ____% have both spouses getting remarried.[1]

More Marriage Facts

These are the reasons people cite for getting married. Put them in the order of most important to you (1) to least important (7) in the column on the left. Then listen as the facilitator tells the actual order and percentages of people who gave these reasons.

Priority		Reasons for getting married	Percent who gave this reason
Mine	World		
		Religious reasons	
		Lifelong commitment	
		Legal rights and benefits	
		Financial stability	
		Love	
		Companionship	
		Children	

How did you compare? Your reasons for getting married may not be far off from the reasons of the rest of the world. That shows that most people, regardless of their beliefs, have similar goals for their marriages.

And now for the most staggering statistics: ____% of first marriages end in divorce, _____% of second marriages end in divorce, and _____% of third marriages end in divorce.

Why do you think the statistics for marital success keep getting worse with each remarriage?

Share your thoughts with the group.

Couples counseling has the highest dropout rate of any type of counseling and the greatest incidence of repeat sessions than any other type of counseling. In fact, according to some reports, couples counseling has a 50% failure rate one-year after counseling ends.[2]

Why do you think that is true?

What are some past or current positive examples of marriage that you have personally witnessed or experienced?

What about negative examples?

Before getting married, did you have fears or con-cerns about it?

Describe what is most important to you when it comes to your marriage.

What advice would you give people who are consider-ing getting married? What do you wish you had known before getting married? Do you have questions about something relating to your marriage now?

The 50% failure rate after counseling makes it look like counseling is a waste of time, but counseling itself is not the problem. During counseling, a high percentage of couples claim that the sessions are helping their marriage. That may be true, but people likely think that if they put in the effort required for counseling, it will be a permanent fix. However, the benefits are temporary because the couples are not equipped with the tools to continue to maintain their marriages, so half of them fail after one year.

When asked when couples should seek professional help for their marriages, Terri Ammirati used the analogy of a fire in a home. She asked: "If you had a fire in your home, would you wait until your house was burning to the ground before you placed the 911 call?"[3] Most people would not, but they tend to ignore these small "fires" in their marriages leaving them nearly destroyed by the time they get help. According to Dr. John Gottman, couples that are unhappy in their marriages wait, on average, six years before seeking counseling.[4]

We believe that a marriage that has burned to the ground can still be restored ... when God is involved. And usually, when something burns down and is rebuilt, it is even better than it was before.

Ezekiel 37:1-10 describes a valley full of dry bones, and the Lord put them back together; He breathed life into the bones and raised a vast army from what was dead and gone. We believe the Lord can restore a marriage that was thought to be dead and gone, but it will probably not be quick, easy, or painless.

It is much quicker, easier, and more painless for couples to perform regular maintenance on their marriages to keep them running in optimal form, strengthened, and prepared for life's challenges.

What do you pray the Lord will restore in your marriage?

1.2 On Your Own

That is why a man leaves his father and mother and is united to his wife, and they become one flesh. Genesis 2:24

Listen, friends, I know not all of you are Bible believers, and the purpose of this course is not to hit you over the head with it, I promise! But hopefully, we can all agree that beneficial suggestions, wisdom, and insight can come from all kinds of sources. This study will pull from many sources. You'll see sources that cover the gamut.

This week may feel more Bible-heavy than the upcoming weeks. Please don't let that discourage you or put a bad taste in your mouth. Bear with us and see what benefit you can glean from all of the sources you'll find here.

Side note: Unless otherwise specified, all scripture references are from the New International Version (NIV).

Marriage is a covenant relationship designed and initiated by God

 Read Genesis 2:18-25.

Why did God create woman?

Now look specifically at verse 24 and fill in the blanks.

"That is why a man _____ his father and mother and ___ _____ to his wife, and they become ____ _____."

This may seem like an odd question, but have you ever had anything surgically removed or repaired, or even delivered a baby? What procedure did you have done? Briefly describe the recovery here.

Even when there is a medical issue that requires something to be surgically removed, there is still injury caused by that removal. There is pain and bleeding involved in even the smallest removal. The doctors have to make sure you aren't on blood thinners so they can cut without fear of you bleeding uncontrollably. Thank God for modern medicine so that we don't have to be aware when it's happening, but it pretty much always hurts for a while afterward.

So, becoming one flesh ... that sounds serious. Does that sound like separation is possible? Well of course it's possible, but does that sound like separation can be painless?

Marriage is designed to be an exclusive relationship between one man and one woman that mirrors God's relationship with His people. This is why you may hear the reference to "the marriage covenant" in Christian teaching.

Read Ephesians 5:28-32.

Laying down our lives does not necessarily mean literally dying for our spouses. Though it could come to that. It means we are willing to sacrifice our own comfort so that the needs of our spouses are met. Someone else is blessed because we sacrificed something.

In these verses, what relationship is compared with that of husband and wife?

When Scripture refers to the church, it's referring to a group of people, not a building or structure. What do you think is the relationship between Christ and the church?

What role does Christ play in the relationship?

What role does the church play?

If you're thinking the church is not fulfilling the role set for it, sadly that is often true. The church is made up of weak and fallible humans, but in today's section, we're referring to the *intention* Christ had in establishing the church. And our prayer for you is that you will see that the church is still alive and active in ways you have never witnessed before.

Marriage is a lifelong commitment

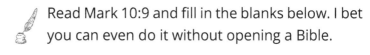 Read Mark 10:9 and fill in the blanks below. I bet you can even do it without opening a Bible.

"Therefore what _____ has joined together, let no one _____."

That pretty much sums it up.

Marriage is a shared identity

Read Matthew 19:5-6.

Sounds familiar right? In this passage, Jesus is quoting a verse we read at the beginning of the home-work. We read Genesis 2:24 where it was first stated, "That is why a man leaves his father and mother and is united to his wife, and they become one flesh." When Jesus quotes something specific from the Old Testament, that must mean it is particularly important.

When a man and a woman get married, they become one. Their identity changes. Not only are the two of them one, but they are joined by God into a strand of three.

God's Knot - Cord of Three Strands

The gold strand represents God (Divinity).

The purple strand represents the groom (Majesty).

The white strand represents the bride (Purity).

Ecclesiastes 4:12 says, "Though one may be overpowered, two can defend themselves. A cord of three strands is not quickly broken."

We will face trials and tribulations in life. Jesus does not promise that we will not face struggles or hardships, but He promises that we will overcome them because He has overcome the world. This is not only individually, but as a couple as well. When there is a strong bond between a husband and a wife and they are bound with Christ, the marriage will persevere.

Pray for your marriage. When we pray for our spouses, or for anyone else, for that matter, our hearts soften towards them. Even if your spouse is less committed to this marriage maintenance journey than you are, your prayers have the power to soften both of your hearts. In fact, even if you aren't normally a believer in the power of prayer and you feel like you don't even know how to do it, simply trying it out can have a powerful effect. If that last sentence speaks to you, let these ten weeks be an experiment. After this class is over, let us know if you noticed a difference in your marriage that seems to be connected with your prayers. Some ideas you can pray about are their job, finances, health, mindset, affection, choices, temptations, relationships, attitudes, and priorities.[5] Jot down which of these things you are praying about, or other things that may be more specific, here.

1.3 Couple Time

That is why a man leaves his father and mother and is united to his wife, and they become one flesh. Genesis 2:24

Look back through the work you did on your own this week and discuss the things that stood out to you as you worked through it.

What did your partner mention that was different than your thoughts?

Pray together. Ask God to bless this work and to bless your marriage. You may come up with your own prayer and speak from the heart, or if you can't think of what to say, you can say this prayer:

God,
We thank You so much for giving us a partner to navigate this life. Most importantly, Lord, we thank You for being at the center of this marriage and reminding us of Your love. We ask for Your blessing over this marriage and may Your hand ever lead us and remind us why You created this union. May we fill the roles that You intended for us and glorify You in all that we do in service to You and to each

other.
In Jesus' name, Amen.

Here's a place to write your own prayer if you want to keep a record of it. At the end of this program, look back on the prayers you've written and see what God has done over these 10 weeks.

Action Plan:

Make time together and name it. Verbally say the words *this is a date*. It makes it real to say something out loud. Say *I love you. I notice you. I see how hard you work*. Say things out loud and give them a name. Language and learning have a strong connection[6]. Keep learning about each other every day.

Pray about the specific things you wrote down at the end of section 1.2.

Look for ways to stand firm with your spouse and live in unity.

Chapter 2

THE MARRIAGE COMMITMENT

2.0 Preparing Your Heart

"Therefore what God has joined together, let no one separate." Mark 10:9

> Objective: This week we will identify the specifics of the commitment we have made and what that commitment requires of us.

From Scott:

I remember that both of my grandfathers would save all kinds of things that I thought were useless. I would ask my grandfather why he kept all that junk, and his response was that he may need it to fix something later. Back then, if something broke they fixed it and continued to use it. Nowadays, we find ourselves in a "throwaway" society; if it's broken, we throw it out and get a new one. Sometimes it's just cheaper and less time-consuming to buy a new one. Of course, there are exceptions. Some of us still try to repair things and keep them going, but most people don't.

Unfortunately, people approach their marriages the same way; if it is broken, throw it out and get a new one. In God's eyes, marriage is a covenant and not a contract, and it should be so in ours as well. Read the objectives of this chapter and start gearing your heart and mind toward discussing *The Marriage Commitment*.

2.1 Group Session

"Therefore what God has joined together, let no one separate." Mark 10:9

Read this paragraph together to get your minds in gear for today's class:

There's a book written with a target audience of business leaders, but the concepts speak directly to marriages as well. In fact, they speak to pretty much everything in life. In James Collins' book *Good to Great: Why Some Companies Make the Leap and Others Don't*[7], the premise is that we get comfortable with the status quo and stop working towards something better. "Things are good," we say. But is that where we want things to be? Did you get married so your life would turn out good? I have a feeling you were dreaming of life being great. Excellent, in fact. So why settle for good when your marriage can be great?

Taking the First Step: You're doing it!

Are you ready for more statistics?

- Couples who receive premarital counseling before their wedding enjoy a _____% higher rate of marital success

- _____% of couples agree to premarital counseling.

- _____% of weddings take place in some type of religious setting.[2]

- Between ____% - _____% of married couples who seek couples counseling see a positive change.[3]

- Divorce proceedings every year involve more than _____ children and increase the likelihood of their growing up in poverty.

- The average cost of a wedding is $_____, but premarital counseling costs less than ____% of this amount.

Before we go on and talk about each other's needs, here's a side note: There are common stereotypes that are normally associated with men or women specifically, but it's not an exact science. I've heard it said that women need to hear *I love you* more than men do. With Scott and me, that's not true. He needs to hear *I love you,* and I need to hear how much he is attracted to me. I have a number of the "His" needs, while Scott has an assortment of the "Her" needs. And some of these needs aren't that big of a deal to either of us. These are generalizations, not expectations or rules; so you shouldn't feel like this is a mold that you have to fit into to be "normal."

Since we've been discussing commitment, what each of you thinks is important, and what you believe is important to your partner, let's take a look at the items in this list from the book *His Needs/Her Needs* by William F. Harley (2013).[10] You may think of more to add to the list or think some of these are untrue, but let's take a look at these and discuss them anyway.

Listen to the brief description the group facilitator gives for each of these needs and think about which of them you have. Write your initials in the margin by each of *your* needs on the list. Then take some time to discuss with the group how you fit with the lists. For example: Are you stronger with one side than the other? Do you have a pretty even mix of needs from both sides? Are you surprised by any of your needs or the description of any of them?

His needs:

- Sexual fulfillment
- Recreational companionship
- An attractive spouse
- Domestic support
- Admiration

Her needs:

- Affection
- Conversation
- Honesty and openness
- Financial stability
- Family commitment

Which of the needs you marked for yourself are most important to you?

Do you know what needs are highest for your partner?

Let's take a look at what Scripture says about fulfilling
each other's needs.

Read Matthew 25:31-46.

To break that down a little bit, what are the
needs mentioned in verses 35-36?

Fill in the missing words from this part of verse 40:
"Truly I tell you, whatever you did for one of the
_____ of these brothers of mine, you did for
_____."

So, in serving one another, we are serving the King!
As you go through this week, try to keep in mind how
you can serve each other through meeting each need
and see how that enriches your own attitude and your
marriage.

Many of the needs in the list we just read are pretty
self-explanatory, but some may have an issue with
the "attractive spouse" need on the husband's list.
Let's take a few minutes to dig into that one. I'm sure
all the women here can agree there are plenty of
times they feel unattractive. But this is not just about
physical beauty.

Men, tell the group some things you find attractive in
a spouse.

Now a question for all of you: Have you ever met someone you found physically attractive and then got to know them and they became completely unattractive to you because of their behaviors, attitudes, or speech? Or has the opposite been true? You met someone you found physically unattractive, but as you got to know them, they became attractive to you?

Having an attractive spouse can follow that same pattern: the ability to become more or less attractive based on behaviors, attitudes, or speech. But physical beauty does come into play as well. In the book of Esther chapter two, we learn Esther was one of the most beautiful women in all of the 127 provinces ruled by King Xerxes. She was so attractive that King Xerxes chose her, above all of the other prospects he had, to become queen. But even as beautiful as she was, before she was allowed to even meet the king, she went through 12 months of beauty treatments.

Now, we're not here to tell you wives that you must spend massive amounts of time and money on beauty treatments, or that you have to wear makeup and perfume and spend hours on your appearance. But we are telling you that putting forth the effort to be attractive to your husband does matter. That may mean exercising and eating right, that may mean wearing more or less makeup, and that may mean changing out of your pajama pants before he comes home from work. The point is, if one of your husband's top needs is an attractive spouse, in order for you to meet that need, you need to make an effort. And husbands, when she makes an effort, it would be great if you would notice and show appreciation.

From Scott: I love it when Carla makes the effort to be attractive for me, but I also do not expect it to be all day, every day; that can be stressful and exhausting. Honestly, guys, we know there are days when we just cannot be all that for her, too. However, as loving husbands, we need to recognize our wives when they make the effort to look attractive for us and give them grace on the days when they are not feeling beautiful by letting them know they are beautiful to us anyway.

The Marriage Commitment Triangle

In the last chapter, we talked about the cord of three strands, known as the 'God Knot.' Here, we want to introduce the concept of the Marriage Commitment Triangle. God is at the apex of the triangle, He is in His position of sovereignty over the relationship. The husband and the wife are at the other points of the triangle, and each point is joined by a relationship bond to each of the other points of the triangle. The idea is that God is committed to the husband and to the wife, the husband is committed to his wife and to God, and the wife is committed to her husband and to God. All of these are straight solid lines in a perfect marriage commitment.

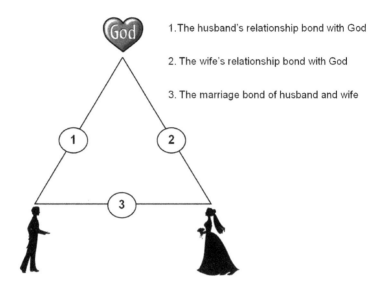

1. The husband's relationship bond with God

2. The wife's relationship bond with God

3. The marriage bond of husband and wife

Make a commitment this week to keep both of your bonds strong in order to protect the stability of the triangle. In other words, spend quality time with God and spend time meeting your spouse's needs. Do you notice that as you and your spouse move closer to God in your relationship, you also become closer to each other?

2.2 On Your Own

"Therefore what God has joined together, let no one separate." Mark 10:9

Do you find it odd that you and your partner have different needs? Are there times when you feel like his or her needs are frivolous or petty?

Let's see what Scripture has to say about that...

Read the parable of the good Samaritan in Luke 10:25-37.

What question prompted Jesus to tell this story?

Who were the two people who passed by the dying man?

Who was the one who stopped and tended to the man's wounds and took care of him?

Let's start with a little history lesson. Jews and Samaritans *hated* each other. And that may be an understatement. The Jewish people, when traveling between Galilee and Judea, would typically go *way* out of their way to avoid Samaria; we're talking miles to the east, across the Jordan River, then north for a lot of miles, then *back* across the river to the west side. This detour added several days to a trip on foot.

Here's a map to give you an idea of the journey:

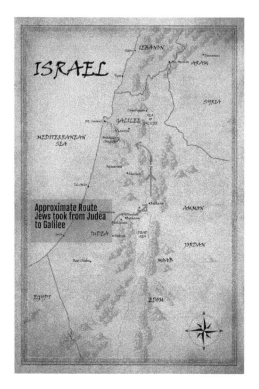

The straighter shot through Samaria was about 70 miles.[11] From Jericho to Nazareth going this round-about way was about 100 miles. On foot. Why would you walk 30 more miles than you had to? The main issue was racism, but there's a long story behind that, and we don't need to go into the details for this study.

Let's get back to the main points of the story:

1) A Jewish man was severely injured to the point that if he were left there much longer he would have died.

2) Two of his countrymen, religious leaders even, passed right by him. Was there something they did

to him that was a problem? No. Actually, it was their *inaction* that showed unkindness.

3) A stranger and arch-enemy stopped to help. What three things did the Samaritan do for the man?

Let's think about what the *Samaritan's* needs were. What do you think this outcast needed? *There are no right or wrong answers here.*

Would Jesus be using this illustration if the Samaritan had seen the injured man and thought, "Hmph! Okay, Buddy, I see you have needs, but I have needs, too. I'll help *you* when I start to see you meeting *my* needs."?

How about if he said, "Here's what *I* need: acceptance, acknowledgment, and how about a kind word when you pass me? So those are the things I'm going to do for *you*."

Ridiculous, right? That's what I'm doing when I either belittle my partner's needs or try to give my partner the things that would fulfill my own needs.

Your spouse is your neighbor more than anyone else in this world. Jesus commands us to love our neighbor and gives this beautiful story of someone showing mercy and taking tender care of a stranger from enemy territory, sacrificing money and time for him, and being willing to risk ridicule and rejection. How much more should I be doing this for my partner?

What is a tangible way you have sacrificed for your spouse this week?

What can you do for your spouse, even when it requires sacrifice from you?

What benefit will you get from that?

As you go through this week, focus on seeing your partner as your neighbor and loving that neighbor. Then write down any results, tangible or intangible, that come from that attitude.

Make a list of things you appreciate about your partner, then when you come together to do the Couple Time, share your list with your partner.

 Pray for your marriage.

2.3 Couple Time

"Therefore what God has joined together, let no one separate." Mark 10:9

Share the list of things you appreciate about your partner.

Look back on the needs list from the group session this week and compare lists. Which of the needs on the list do both of you share?

Which needs does your partner have that you need to be more intentional about fulfilling?

In the *On Your Own* section this week, we talked about the Good Samaritan. It is a story of strangers and we're talking about our life partners. It's of course different, and oddly it sometimes seems more challenging to be kind to those closest to us than it is to be kind to strangers, but that's why we are here. We want to step up our intimate relationships and take care of them daily so that they will thrive.

Let's take a look at another Scripture talking about strangers. Remember, whatever we do for strangers should be menial compared to what we do for our partners.

Read Hebrews 13:1-6 together.

Now let's dissect this passage a little.

In verse 2, what does it say we should show to strangers, and potentially to angels?

There are several other things listed that we should be doing to honor God and others. And an important statement is made in verse 6. Who is our helper?

Now jump over to Proverbs 11:25. Fill in these blanks:

"A _____ person will _____; whoever _____ others will be _____."

One more scripture for today: go to 2 Corinthians 9:6-9 and read it together.

In verse 6, we see sowing _____ results in reaping _____, and sowing _____ re- sults in reaping _____.

Now fill in these blanks from verse 8:

"And God is able to bless you _____, so that in _____ things at _____ times, having _____ that you need, you will abound in _____ good work."

So, after today's session, here's what we know:

- We need to be honoring and serving each other generously.

- The Lord will give us all that we need to do so.

- He is our helper in all our endeavors.

- Knowing these things, how can we go wrong?

Take time to pray together and ask God to bless this work you're doing and to bless your marriage. You may come up with your own prayer and speak from the heart, or if you can't think of what to say, you can say this prayer:

Heavenly Father,
Thank You for bringing us together and for Your commitment to our marriage. We pray, Lord, for Your blessing and protection upon this marriage and that You would continually guide and strengthen us in our commitment. Father, we ask for the provision of Your love to flow through our hearts and that we will be strengthened in service to each other. Finally, Lord, we pray that You would speak to our hearts what You want us to take from this lesson, and please prepare us for the next as we continue to work toward maintaining a healthy marriage.
In Jesus' name, Amen

Here's a place to write your own prayer if you want to keep a record of it. At the end of this program, look back on the prayers you've written and see what God has done over these 10 weeks.

Action Plan:

Pay attention to your spouse's needs and make efforts to meet them. Do something every day, even if it is small, to meet a need.

Tell your spouse how you appreciate them. Make it a habit.

Watch how meeting each need enriches your own attitude and your marriage.

Chapter 3

EFFECTIVE COMMUNICATION

3.0 Preparing Your Heart

"Do not let any unwholesome talk come out of your mouths, but only what is helpful for building others up according to their needs, that it may benefit those who listen." Ephesians 4:29

Objective: This week we will create a plan for developing and maintaining effective communication in our marriages.

From Carla:

I remember when I first started teaching. I had a roommate who was a kindergarten teacher, and I loved all the little expressions they would say to remind themselves of the kind of behavior that was expected of them. One of my favorites that has popped back into my head many times is "Watch your words."

These three words are so wise. The words we allow to come out of our mouths are out there forever. We can't un-say them, and the recipient of those words can't un-hear them. I can think back on conversations more than thirty years ago and remember what specific people said to me, for better or for worse. I can remember some things word for word. Can you?

Knowing that is true, we must learn to be more deliberate with what we allow to come out of our mouths. James 3:2 says that if we can control our tongues perfectly, we will be perfect in all other aspects. Can you imagine that? There are two important inferences that can be taken from that verse: the tongue is powerfully capable of corruption, and taming the tongue empowers us to gain control of our other weaknesses. So if you haven't been working on this already, we encourage you to start this week: Watch Your Words.

3.1 Group Session

"Do not let any unwholesome talk come out of your mouths, but only what is helpful for building others up according to their needs, that it may benefit those who listen." Ephesians 4:29

I would like to expand a little bit on what Carla said in this week's preparation about controlling our words. One good book that I used in one of my counseling classes was Dr. James C. Petersen's *Why Don't We Listen Better? Communicating & Connecting in Relationships.* At one point, Dr. Petersen presents a physical analogy of our communication by using the brain, heart, and stomach. Common sense would have us think that using our heart and our brain in communication would be effective, but many times we have "gut" responses too, and those can often be impulsive in nature. Imagine these impulsive ideas building and expanding the stomach. As this happens, the heart is compressed, the brain is compressed, and both become less effective in managing communication. Eventually, there is no more room left, the mouth is forced open to relieve the pressure, and all of our "stomach talk" comes flying out.[12] As Carla said, we need to be more deliberate as we watch our words.

Now, let's look at several key techniques for communicating effectively in your marriage:

1. Be intentional

You may say, "But I'm spontaneous." Then be intentionally spontaneous! Make a commitment to use effective communication and follow these guidelines listed, but feel free to be spontaneous about how you do it.

Think about how your spouse reacts or feels when you meet one of his or her needs. When it comes to communication, our biggest need is to be understood. We may be *hearing* what our spouses are saying, but to be intentional, we must *listen* to what our spouses are saying.

2. Use more "I" statements and fewer "You" statements. When you communicate your needs to your partner, focus on the way you feel by making statements that start with "I feel," and avoid statements that feel accusatory. Especially avoid using *always* and *never* in your statements. You should avoid saying things like "You always..." or "You never..." Let's practice. In these two examples, circle Y for things that you should say, do, or think, and circle N for things you should just keep to yourself.

Y/N – I feel lonely when you go out with friends and leave me home alone.

Y/N – You always go out with your friends, and you don't even care that we haven't had time together.

Now you try. Come up with a statement that is beneficial to say to your spouse and one that is better kept to yourself.

Y – I feel...

N – You always...

3. Be specific

- Here's a note to the wives: it is *so easy* for women to make our husbands feel like failures, especially when we have unrealistic expectations like, "I shouldn't have to tell him I want him to switch the laundry over. He should just know and do it without me prompting him." Trust me, he doesn't know. Am I right, husbands? What can you do to encourage him and lift him up, rather than squashing his ego? Could it be something as simple as verbalizing the need that you want him to fill? Most likely, he will be HAPPY to do that for you!

- Husbands, I'm sure we could come up with an example of something you should be specific about to your wives too, right? "Why can't she just move the seat back after she drives my car?" There are other things that irritate you, I'm sure.

- Jot down something you need to be more specific about with your spouse here:

4. Avoid mind-reading – Give your spouse the benefit of the doubt. Don't assume your spouse's thoughts or predict their behavior.

Y/N – He knows it bugs me to have dishes in the sink. He probably left that plate there to irritate me.

Y/N – He must be really busy or he would have put that dish in the dishwasher. I'll move it for him. That is something small I can do for him that doesn't cost me anything.

5. Express negative feelings constructively

- Be kind. "Perhaps you will forget tomorrow the kind words you say today, but the recipient may cherish them over a lifetime." - Dale Carnegie

- When have you ever vented about someone and then walked away from the conversation loving them even more? Write about that here.

- You couldn't think of anything could you? When you vent about anything, you typically become more agitated. Next time you're tempted to vent about something your spouse did or didn't do, try letting it go instead. Go back to some of the other principles listed here and see if you feel more calm as a result.

- We would never tell you to bottle up all of your negative thoughts and never tell your spouse, but it may be best to hold off on expressing something negative, even constructively, until you both are further from the situation. Judge wisely when it should be shared and do so with kindness.

6. Listen without being defensive

Y/N – You don't like when I leave the toilet seat up? Well, I don't like when you leave the toothpaste cap off!

Y/N – You hate it when I talk like a duck? I'm sorry about that. It's such a habit, but I'll try to remember not to do it because you don't like it.

Yes, that's a silly example, but it hopefully gets the point across. Jot down a non-defensive response to a recent criticism you've heard from your spouse:

7. Freely express positive feelings

- Affirming your spouse is critical to a healthy marriage.

- **If you don't get anything else from this chapter, get this: Your spouse needs to hear praise from you! Pour it on. Say "I love you" often, and praise the smallest things.**

- On the flip side, when your spouse is saying "I love you" often and praising the smallest things, don't be skeptical or cynical about it. Yes, it may seem excessive, but this exercise is something that we know from experience truly works. Being overly loving and positive will rub off on your attitude and you will feel it more in your soul. If nothing else, it will give you something to smile about.

8. LISTEN!

Did we mention "listen" before (see #6)? We just cannot emphasize how important listening is to effective communication. Please keep in mind that hearing and listening are not synonymous. We must actively listen in order to understand what our spouses are trying to say. And guys, we DO NOT have to fix things every time. Yes, it is going to be tough to keep our cape firmly tucked inside our shirts, but sometimes our wives just want us to be there for them, to listen, and to be supportive. Carla reassures me that our wives WILL tell us if they need us to swoop in and save the day. With that said, let's look at some key listening techniques that both husbands and wives can apply.

Dr. Petersen offers 33 tips throughout his book that I mentioned in the opening. I will summarize some important ones here:[13]

- Acknowledge the speaker by employing words, tone, and body language that reassures them you are present in the conversation.

- Repeat accurately and admit when you do not understand - feel free to gently interrupt to ask for clarification.

- Resist the urge to immediately answer, solve, or offer advice.

- Listen without agreeing, disagreeing, advising, or defending, as these are actually "talking" techniques. Even if you are doing this in your mind, and not aloud, you are distracted from active listening.

3.2 On Your Own

"Do not let any unwholesome talk come out of your mouths, but only what is helpful for building others up according to their needs, that it may benefit those who listen." Ephesians 4:29

The homework this week will feel a little like a continuation of the group session, and it may feel a little redundant. Get this, though: *If you don't have good communication as a couple, you can't do what it takes to improve on any other areas of your relationship.* The foundational issue for marital discord is poor communication.

So here our list continues:

9. Do not put your spouse on the defensive

- We mentioned in number 6 to listen without getting defensive, but that is easier to do if you are communicating with each other without accusing.

- What is something you have said in the past in a way that feels accusatory?

- How can you say that same thing without making your spouse feel defensive?

- Does timing factor into whether that statement will be taken well? Should you have chosen a better time to say it?

10. Avoid generalizations - "You do it all the time!" "You're never available to help when I need you." Can you think of any others?

Bitterness, resentment, disappointment, or disapproval need to be conveyed ... but do so with gentleness and patience. (And before you do so, ask yourself if you're being selfish. Is what you want to say helpful to the relationship in any way? Or will it just make you feel better? Will it really?

Effective communication is important when:

1. Discussing feelings

2. Discussing issues

3. Making decisions (routine, important, and emergency)

4. Keeping your spouse in-the-loop

5. Managing expectations

6. Listening for understanding

7. Listening to God

Assignment: Be intentional this week about affirming your spouse, minimizing criticism by speaking kindly and constructively, and following the general guidelines set forth in this chapter. Journal about the experience with your efforts below. How does it make you feel? How does it impact your relationship?

Pray for your marriage.

3.3 Couple Time

"Do not let any unwholesome talk come out of your mouths, but only what is helpful for building others up according to their needs, that it may benefit those who listen." Ephesians 4:29

This week, your couple time assignment is to go on a date. Here are the parameters for your date:

- Go somewhere you can talk – maybe a park, a quiet dinner, a walk, etc.

- Go somewhere with minimal interruptions and distractions.

- Spend the majority of your time (at least 75%) talking about positive or neutral things.

- Reminisce about fun or funny times you've had together: possibly big things like vacations, the birth of your children, or the events of your wedding day, but also small things like board games you used to play together or that one time you went to a dinner that turned into a comedy of errors.

Use the space below to briefly describe what you did for your date this week.

Take time to pray together and ask God to bless this work you're doing and to bless your marriage. You may come up with your own prayer and speak from the heart, or if you can't think of what to say, you can say this prayer:

> Holy Lord,
> Effective communication is so vital to our well-being and we are so thankful that we have a direct link to You through prayer and that You respond in many ways. Father, please move in us through Your Holy Spirit providing us words to speak which reflect love and kindness to each other in a way that strengthens our marital bond. Please help our actions support our positive communication as we seek to encourage others in their lives and marriages as well.
> In Jesus' name, Amen.

Here's a place to write your own prayer if you want to keep a record of it. At the end of this program, look back on the prayers you've written and see what God has done over these 10 weeks.

Action Plan:

Watch your words. Be deliberate about how you talk to and about your spouse.

Use more energy on affirming your spouse. Speak positive, uplifting words.

Avoid criticizing and negative speech.

Go on a date!

Chapter 4

DEALING WITH CONFLICT: RECOGNIZING CONFLICT STYLES

4.0 Preparing Your Heart

"Be completely humble and gentle, be patient, bearing with one another in love. Make every effort to keep the unity of the Spirit through the bond of peace." Ephesians 4:2-3

Objective: This week we will identify conflict styles and practice healthy conflict management attitudes and skills that will improve our relationship.

From Scott:

Do you or someone you love, perhaps your spouse, deal with a high level of anxiety? The apostle Paul wrote in Philippians 4:6 that we should not be anxious about anything; instead, we should take all of our concerns to God in prayer. I personally deal with a high level of anxiety, and I can tell you that it is not always easy to calm my own fears. Most often our fears are heightened when we are not in control of the situation, such as being a passenger in a vehicle ... or plane. Even though I have never flown a plane before, I bet I would have less anxiety flying a plane myself than being a passenger. Although, the other passengers might have something to say about that switch.

There is a big problem when anxiety has complete control over you and controls your responses. One cold blustery day while Carla and I were traveling to our son's basketball tournament, I experienced a hostile takeover from my anxiety that I wish I could get out of my mind, but I will share it with you anyway. Carla was driving and noticed a cow running through the field that she thought was amusing and said "Hey, look at that little cow!" Just as she said that a huge gust of wind came up and majorly rocked our car. However, my anxiety took over and told me 'This is it! This is the big crash that is going to kill us all!' My ridiculous response was, "You should keep your eyes on the road instead of watching the cows!" As soon as those words left my mouth with that tone, I could feel guilt and regret in my soul.

This is a good analogy for my conflict style; I am the typical avoider. When it comes to conflict, I hold it all in until it reaches a fever pitch, and then I say something stupid. In the above recollection, I should have been praying for comfort from my anxiety. I should have taken steps to avoid the buildup inside. Instead, my internal conflict with anxiety boiled over and I said something that deeply hurt Carla. This week, let's take a look at *Recognizing Conflict Styles,* because this is an important step in learning to deal with conflict.

4.1 Group Session

"Be completely humble and gentle, be patient, bearing with one another in love. Make every effort to keep the unity of the Spirit through the bond of peace." Ephesians 4:2-3

If you have conflict in your marriage, there is one thing you can know for sure: You are normal! A lack of conflict does not equal happiness. It means there is denial and avoidance happening, and there will most certainly be an underlying current of discontent that can only lead to bigger issues in the future.

One of the goals of this class is to build a neutral zone for discussing issues that are hard to discuss otherwise. Having a common vocabulary for defining attitudes, actions, and reasons for those attitudes and actions is important; that vocabulary will make it easier for you to communicate clearly and work through conflicts. It will be as if you are speaking the same language! Let's get into some of the "language" about conflict...

There are three personality types that come up when discussing conflict: avoiders, volatiles, and validators. Read these lists of attributes and check off the ones that apply to you to determine which category most closely defines your conflict style:

Avoiders:

- They are people-pleasers.

- They have a fear of upsetting others.

- They feel like conflict is a lose-lose situation and make any excuse to avoid it.

- They have a fear of expressing themselves.

- They silently resent things that do not resolve.

- They may silently accumulate grievances, annoyances, and problems only to let it all out in one outburst – a lack of response is a response in itself.

Volatiles:

- They experience both positive and negative emotions very easily, and sometimes to extremes.

- They continue to actively engage in the conflict and will not withdraw.

- They listen to other points of view but still fight for their own perspective.

- They do not compromise.

- They can still remain warm and loving and do not want to intentionally inflict pain.

- They may engage in playful teasing.

- They can be bluntly honest.

Validators:

- They listen intently to others.

- They show support and concern for others.

- They display ease and calm.

- They practice self-control.

- They always search for compromise.

Of course, you probably will not fit squarely into one of the above lists. Basically, everyone has elements of two or more categories, and some days you may waver between which one is most prominent in you. One thing I hope you notice about these lists is that there are strengths and weaknesses in each of them.

Which of these three do you identify with the most?

Which of the three is your secondary identifier?

Five Types of Couple Conflict:

Couples fall into one of five categories when it comes to how they deal with conflict.

Conflict Avoiders

- These couples use minimal persuasion attempts and emphasize common ground.

- There is a balance between independence and interdependence with clear boundaries.

- They are separate people with separate interests.

Volatile Couples

- These couples are intensely emotional.

- They use persuasion throughout their discussions.

- They love to debate and argue for entertainment, but they are not disrespectful or insulting.

Validating Couples

- These couples have interactions characterized by ease and calm.

- They are somewhat expressive but emphasize supporting and understanding each other's points of view.

- They are empathetic.

Hostile Couples

- These couples are made up of one volatile, typically the husband, and one avoider, typically the wife.

- They are expressive with a high level of defensiveness, criticism, whining, and contempt.

Hostile-Detached Couples

- These couples are made up of one validator and one volatile.

- They are mutually frustrated and standoffish or default to a stalemate.

- They often take shots at one another at the time of conflict but are emotionally detached and resigned.

Be thinking about which of these five categories describes your marriage relationship; it will come up during the couple time this week.

Three of the above categories of couples fall on the positive side of conflict management. They are the first three listed, Conflict Avoiders, Volatile Couples, and Validating Couples.

If you fall into one of the negative categories, don't lose heart. You aren't destined to stay there if you have the will to make the change, especially when you are working together toward a common goal. Scott and I started off pretty solidly in the Hostile Couples category, and it was not fun. Then, as we both worked with determination to improve our relationship, we started inching toward the Validating Couples bracket, which is so much more satisfying.[14]

What does the Bible say about conflict?

I Kings 4 says King Solomon's wisdom was unsurpassed. Let's see what he has to say. Read these scriptures aloud:

Proverbs 15:1 and 15:18

Think of a situation where someone spoke harshly with you. Did you feel calm or angry? How did your response affect the rest of the conversation?

Now think of a situation where you spoke harshly to someone. How did you feel afterward? What kind of response did you get? How did you feel after the response?

Think of a situation where you or someone else spoke gently or patiently and the tensions eased. What was that like?

 Read Proverbs 16:22.

What is the opposite of understanding or prudence?

What happens to those who do not have understanding?

 Read Proverbs 17:14.

Why shouldn't you start an argument?

Have you ever seen footage of or witnessed a dam failure? If so, what happened? If not, what do you think would happen?

 Proverbs 21:19 warns us that it is "better to live in a desert than with a quarrelsome and ill-tempered wife." Also, Proverbs 19:13 com-

pares a quarrelsome wife to constant dripping. I hesi-
tate to say a quarrelsome husband would be that way
too. Scott just wonders why such a wise man would
be "taking shots" at his wife. Perhaps Solomon was
speaking from experience. Was his wife quarrelsome?
What was causing her to be quarrelsome? Is it her
own negative attitude? Did his behavior help or hurt
the situation?

Side note: Nagging can sometimes be a way
to try to push your spouse to "be better."
But, it is the wrong way to accomplish
that. More about this type of criticism is
in chapter 5.

Is there a correlation to what Paul would later
write? In Ephesians 5:22 he wrote, "Wives, submit yourselves to your own husbands as you do
to the Lord," and in Ephesians 5:25, "Husbands, love
your wives, just as Christ loved the church and gave
himself up for her." If a husband is loving, his wife is
less likely to be quarrelsome. If a wife is respectful,
her husband is more likely to be loving. If a husband
is loving his wife as Christ loved the church, she will
want to submit to him. It is important to understand
that submission is not a show of weakness. The best
way for a husband to get his wife to submit is by being
the husband he is called to be, not by trying to force
her to submit.

Side note: Men are commanded to love their
wives with the obvious understanding that
the command is only directed towards their
wives and not all women. In the same way,

women are commanded to submit to their husbands, not to all men.

Speaking of Paul, he had quite a bit to teach about living at peace with one another. Read Romans 12:6-8. Then read verse 8 again. What gifts are listed here that come in handy in our relationships with our spouses? What attitude should we have when using our gifts?

 Read Philippians 2:3-7.

What is Paul asking us to do here?

Think of at least one time when you were being self-ish. How would it have turned out differently if you followed the instructions from this passage?

Complete the following three passages of Scripture:

1. Philippians 2:14: "Do everything without _____ or _____."

2. Ephesians 4:15: "Instead, speaking the _____ in _____, we will grow to become in every respect the mature body of him who is the head, that is, _____."

3. Romans 12:17: "Do not repay anyone _____ _____ _____. Be careful to do what is _____ in the eyes of _____."

How do these passages relate to Paul's message of being at peace with one another?

How can we best exemplify peace in the face of conflict?

The tools in this chapter are important for use on a regular basis. They are not just for occasions when things get bad between you and your spouse. Keep them handy. As you work through the homework this week, pay attention to the skills you need to develop for regular maintenance of your marriage.

4.2 On Your Own

"Be completely humble and gentle; be patient, bearing with one another in love. Make every effort to keep the unity of the Spirit through the bond of peace." Ephesians 4:2-3

A common thought is that conflict is always negative and should be avoided at all costs, but that is not true.

Our goal is understanding and managing conflict, not avoiding it.

1. Conflict can arise when one person's perceptions, desires, ideas, or values differ from those of another. What differences do you encounter regularly in your marriage?

2. Conflict can be over something trivial or about something carrying more significance. List a few trivial and not-so-trivial sources of conflict in your marriage.

3. Conflict can start out with some discomfort and lead to stronger feelings of anger or hurt if not managed. What are some pitfalls of unmanaged conflict?

4. Conflict can strengthen relationships and lead to understanding ... that is why it is important for couples to "fight fairly." List some rules you can think of for fighting fairly:

 Read 1 Corinthians 13:4-7. How does this help you approach conflict?

This was mentioned at the beginning of Chapter 3, but let's look at it again; read James 3:3-6. Notice the small but powerful things the tongue is compared to: a bit in a horse's mouth, a rudder of a large ship, and a spark that causes a forest fire. Consider carefully how you use your speech. Your tongue is very powerful.

What needs to change about the way you use your speech?

Pray for your marriage.

4.3 Couple Time

"Be completely humble and gentle, be patient, bearing with one another in love. Make every effort to keep the unity of the Spirit through the bond of peace." Ephesians 4:2-3

Look back at the group session and see how you each identified, whether as avoiders, volatiles, or validators.

Now, which of the categories under "Five Types of Couple Conflict" does that put your relationship in?

Are you happy with where you landed? If not, jot down some ideas of how you can work on improving your conflict style.

Feel free to discuss your individual responses from the *On Your Own* section.

Take time to pray together and ask God to bless this work you're doing and to bless your marriage. You may come up with your own prayer and speak from the heart, or if you can't think of what to say, you can say this prayer:

> Glorious Father,
> Conflict is a part of all of our lives. Not all conflict is bad, but it is how we respond to it and how we recover from it that determines the impact that it has on our lives. Lord, You promised us in Scripture that You would use any situation for the good of those that love You. Father God, we ask for Your presence in the face of conflict that you would help keep us calm and act with kindness and love to one another. Please use this lesson to teach us ways to effectively manage conflict. Please give

us the words that build one another up and use our conflict in a way that promotes growth in this marriage relationship. Also, Lord, in situations where conflict has caused damage, please offer us the gift of recovery and healing.
In Jesus' name, Amen.

Here's a place to write your own prayer if you want to keep a record of it. At the end of this program, look back on the prayers you've written and see what God has done over these 10 weeks.

Action Plan:

Speak gently with each other.

Do not start arguments.

Wives show respect to your husbands. Husbands show love to your wives. Do this even if you are not yet receiving the love or respect you want. See how it changes the dynamic of your relationship.

Chapter 5

DEALING WITH CONFLICT: BEHAVIORS, RESPONSES, AND RESOLUTIONS

5.0 Preparing Your Heart

"Therefore, as God's chosen people, holy and dearly loved, clothe yourselves with compassion, kindness, humility, gentleness and patience. Bear with each other and forgive one another if any of you has a grievance against someone. Forgive as the Lord forgave you." Colossians 3:12-13

Objective: This week we will identify and demonstrate conflict resolution skills that will be successful and manageable for our marriages.

From Scott:

Have you ever heard of the term *imposter syndrome*? It is a psychological phenomenon where we doubt our skills, accomplishments, or even our calling, which leads to a persistent fear of failure or being exposed as a fraud. In other words, we begin to believe that we're not good enough, we're in the wrong place, or we can't do anything right. Have you ever had a parent, child, teacher, boss, friend, or spouse make you feel like you can't do anything right? You work so hard and, yet, you get more attention for what you did wrong or what you forgot to do than what you accomplished. Sometimes it's not deliberate, but it makes us feel degraded, nonetheless.

I'll venture to say that all of us have been made to feel that way at some point in our lives. Why? Because imposter syndrome is a tool that the devil uses to steer us away from happily serving and loving others. It may be the way someone says something or it may be the devil whispering negative ideas into our ears. Our response or behaviors to this can often be driven by fear, insecurity, frustration, hurt, or anger. We instinctively lash out instead of responding constructively and lovingly. God has called us all to be His and to serve our families in love, but the devil is doing everything he can to disrupt our lives. Conflict is inevitable. So, we need to recognize and understand the appropriate and effective *Behaviors, Responses, and Resolutions* when *Dealing with Conflict*.

5.1 Group Session

"Therefore, as God's chosen people, holy and dearly loved, clothe yourselves with compassion, kindness, humility, gentleness and patience. Bear with each other and forgive one another if any of you has a grievance against someone. Forgive as the Lord forgave you." Colossians 3:12-13

In the previous chapter, we discussed some of the categories of conflict. Our intent was to get you thinking about these in order to recognize how you approach conflict. In this chapter, we will take a look at how to recognize conflict behaviors and how to manage them positively.

Here are some common tactics and responses during arguments that can put a strain on marriages.

Negative tactics:

- **Criticism** includes attacking the character of one's spouse.

- **Contempt** includes disrespect, mocking, sarcasm, ridicule, and scoffing.

Negative responses:

- **Defensiveness** includes offering excuses, playing the victim card, and reversal of blame, and is typically a response to criticism.

- **Stonewalling** is marked withdrawal and evasiveness and is a common response to contempt. Do not think that silence is a lack of response. **Silence is a response.**

Positive alternatives:

- Instead of criticism ... **use "I" statements** to express a positive need.

- Instead of contempt ... **build a culture of appreciation** by remembering the positive qualities of your spouse and finding gratitude in positive actions.

- Instead of defensiveness ... **take responsibility** by accepting your spouse's perspective, and offer an apology for wrongdoing.

- Instead of stonewalling ... **take a break** and spend some time with something that is physiologically self-soothing and distracting (take a walk, go for a swim, or ride a bike).

Practice:

Think of an example of a criticism of your spouse.

- Reword your concern using an "I" statement.

- How does Proverbs 12:18 help us here?

Think about the characteristics or mannerisms of your spouse that bug you. Now think of the things you absolutely love about your spouse.

- Would you rather lose both qualities or keep both?

- What is your mood toward your spouse when you think about the negative?

- What is your mood toward your spouse when you think about the positive?

- How does Matthew 7:3 help us here?

Think about a time when you became defensive about something your spouse said.

- Was it true?

- If so, how could you have humbly taken responsibility for it? If not, how could you have responded more positively?

- How does James 1:9 help us here?

This may come as a shock, but conflict does not begin with the first action; it actually begins with the response. So the actions of one spouse do not create conflict. The response from the other spouse does.

Think about this for a second. Say, for instance, that I like to sing out loud in the shower. If my wife is ok with it, then there is no conflict between us, right? If my wife is not home and I sing out loud, is there any conflict? Howling dogs aside, there is still no conflict between my wife and me. Now, if my wife were in one of her online lessons or sleeping or studying, my belting out a Sinatra tune in the shower most likely would cause some conflict. However, the point is that the conflict did not begin with the inception of my singing, but how my singing was received.

For those exceptions-to-every-rule people: yes, if I know my wife is sleeping or in a lesson and I deliberately start singing, then I have indeed initiated the conflict with my singing.

Let us take a look at the five stages of conflict:

1. The *Latent Stage*, is where the potential for conflict begins and is typically sparked by an imbalance between needs and availability, desire for control over activities, or divergent goals. This stage is characterized by "unstable" peace.

2. The *Perceived Stage* is when one or more parties becomes aware that the conflict exists. This is the emergence of conflict.

3. The *Felt Stage* is when the emotions of the affected parties, such as tension, stress, and anxiety, begin to affect interaction within the relationship. This stage is when the escalation of conflict begins.

4. The *Manifest Stage* is when the actions and behaviors of the parties begin to frustrate one another. In other words, this is when the internalized conflict emerges and draws in the other party.

5. The *Aftermath Stage* is the outcome of the conflict and is marked by a de-escalation of the conflict, either through resolution or dissolution. [1]

Can you think of a conflict between you and your spouse that is in the latent stage right now? *(Trick question! If you can think of the conflict, it is already in the perceived stage.)*

In reference to my example of singing in the shower, what might the perceived stage look like?

How about the felt stage?

We believe that the felt stage is the key to the conflict. Why do you think that is the case?

We stated earlier that "a lack of conflict does not equal happiness," and "there is denial and avoidance happening" if a couple believes that they have no conflict in their marriage. In what stages might their conflicts be stuck and why?

5.2 On Your Own

"Therefore, as God's chosen people, holy and dearly loved, clothe yourselves with compassion, kindness, humility, gentleness and patience. Bear with each other and forgive one another if any of you has a grievance against someone. Forgive as the Lord forgave you." Colossians 3:12-13

Forgiveness is a critical component in dealing with conflict. Prayer helps. Stormie Omartian[16] has written several books along the lines of building a strong prayer life and praying for others. In *The Power of a Praying Wife*, she talked about two important components of a happy marriage: conflict and forgiveness. Conflict is a component of any marriage, but forgiveness is a critical difference that makes a marriage happier. Let's take a look at some scripture that can help us make better choices in dealing with conflict in our relationships.

 Proverbs 29:11: "Fools give full vent to their rage, but the wise bring calm in the end."

Based on this scripture, and assuming you want calm in your marriage, what should you avoid?

You may have responded *rage* or *venting*. Hopefully, your anger is not getting to the point of rage, although there may be times when you would describe your feelings that way. But, even when you are so angry you feel like you're going to explode, this proverb tells you to control your vent.

Have you ever used a pressure cooker? There is a valve on the top of modern pressure cookers that keeps the pressure in, and when the food is finished cooking, you can choose the way you want to release the pressure: by manual release or natural release. You can open that valve and a burst of steam will come spewing out, or the pressure will slowly release from that valve on its own over a longer period of time. If you do the quick release and your face or hand or any other part of your body is near that vent, you risk serious injury. If you allow time for natural release, you can hover right around the pressure cooker, and you probably won't even notice it's happening.

Relate this pressure cooker analogy to the verse we read earlier from Proverbs 29:11. In your own words write how they relate to each other:

What can you do differently in your interactions with your spouse that will bring calm to your marriage?

 Pray for your marriage.

5.3 Couple Time

"Therefore, as God's chosen people, holy and dearly loved, clothe yourselves with compassion, kindness, humility, gentleness and patience. Bear with each other and forgive one another if any of you has a grievance against someone. Forgive as the Lord forgave you." Colossians 3:12-13

This couple time is a little different from most. There is more reading than answering questions, but bear with us here and hopefully this will speak to you both.

We mentioned Queen Esther in chapter 2. Let's go back to that story.

Queen Esther showed wisdom in the way she related to her husband. To be fair, her husband was a powerful king known to be extreme at times. We are not saying this example is there in Scripture as a *command* for how we relate to our spouses or how women should relate to their husbands, but we see wisdom and sensitivity that may be something we could emulate in sensitive times.

If you don't know the story, you should read it. We're just talking about one little part here, but you need a little background information to understand it.

Esther was a Jew, but no one in the king's household knew. Sadly, the king's right-hand man, Haman, was an "enemy of the Jews," according to Esther 3:10. Haman sent orders in the king's name to have all of the Jews in all of the provinces killed. So Esther had to do something. She had to talk to the king to tell him she was a Jew and to alert him to what was happening to her people.

You probably know you can't just walk up to a king and start a conversation. There was a process that had to be followed, even for the queen. If Esther went about it wrong, she could be killed immediately. She risked her life by approaching the king without his invitation, but he loved her, so when she approached, he raised his scepter to show she was welcome. He also told her she could have whatever she wished.

Esther didn't just blurt out her predicament, though. Instead, she invited the king and Haman to a banquet she had prepared. After enjoying the banquet, the king asked her what she wanted and offered her up to half his kingdom again. But Esther still didn't feel the time was right, so she invited them to return the next day.

As before, after the banquet, the King offered Esther half of his kingdom and asked for her request, and this time she finally asked him to spare her people. When the king found out Haman was responsible for her distress, he was enraged. I'll let you read the book of Esther to find out the rest of the story.

By now you may be wondering what this has to do with our modern-day marriages.

In this chapter, we are talking about our behaviors, how we respond to conflict and to each other, and how we can resolve conflict. Here are the facts from our story:

1. Esther had needs that only her husband could resolve.

2. Esther was intimidated and fearful about approaching her husband, the king.

3. Before approaching her husband, Esther spent 3 days fasting and thinking about it.

4. Esther spoke to her husband twice before sharing her concerns with him.

5. Her husband the king was open to listening to Esther's needs.

6. Esther prepared a banquet for the king — twice — before sharing her distress with him.

Again, what does this have to do with us? Here are some nuggets we may gain from this story:

1. Often, we have needs or problems that only our spouses can resolve.

2. Sometimes it is intimidating to talk to our spouses about our needs or problems.

3. Sometimes, we need to think for a day or more about what we need to talk about to our spouses.

4. Sometimes, when we speak to our spouses, we realize it's still not the right time to discuss our situation. It is helpful to choose carefully how and when to approach our spouses about sensitive subjects.

5. We should always be willing to listen to whatever is bothering our spouses.

6. Sometimes doing something nice for our spouses will make it easier to have a conversation about our situation.

Take time to pray together and ask God to bless this work you're doing and to bless your marriage. You may come up with your own prayer and speak from the heart, or if you can't think of what to say, you can say this prayer:

Holy Lord,
You have such compassion for Your people. We are recipients of Your grace and

mercy, yet we cannot comprehend the unlimited breadth of Your patience. If we only had a grain of the kindness, love, and empathy for others that You have for us, that would make an amazing impact on the lives of others. Lord, grant us the patience to interact with one another in kindness and love, especially with our spouses. Give us a heart of empathy, words of compassion, and a love that conquers all forces that come against our marriage and our trust in You.

In Jesus' name, Amen.

Here's a place to write your own prayer if you want to keep a record of it. At the end of this program, look back on the prayers you've written and see what God has done over these 10 weeks.

Action Plan:

Avoid criticism, contempt, stonewalling, and defensiveness.

Forgive each other when conflicts arise.

Take responsibility when you are in the wrong or have hurt your spouse (even if you were right).

Be open with your spouse about whatever is distressing to you.

Be willing to listen with gentleness to your spouse when they need to share something that is distressing to them.

Chapter 6

Defending the Integrity of Your Union: Outside Forces

6.0 Preparing Your Heart

"Give honor to marriage, and remain faithful to one another in marriage. God will surely judge people who are immoral and those who commit adultery."
Hebrews 13:4 NLT

Objective: This week we will create an action plan for protecting our marriage from negative influences or attacks.

From Scott:

As Carla and I created this workbook, we injected some of our own personal experiences into the material. Over the years, I have thought, 'If I had done this or that or avoided this or that, then I would not have had failed marriages.' Those failed marriages negatively impacted my life, my exes, my children and other family members, and my friends. God often reminds me that I am not the sum of my past mistakes. Rather, He can use those past mistakes for good. Sometimes when people give you advice about life and you know they have not encountered the same experiences as you, it's easy to shrug it off and say they don't know what I am going through. Please understand that Carla and I have been through failed relationships and we want to help you.

This chapter is significant for me because outside forces have been the catalyst for my failed marriages. Notice that I did not say that they were the *causes* of my failed marriages because I firmly believe that external forces only exacerbate the internal struggles in marriages. Internal problems cause gaps in the relationships that permit external forces to gain a foothold and widen those gaps, preventing them from closing. That is why a seemingly innocent or professional friendship can suddenly take a turn toward something more destructive. There are many external things that can negatively impact the success of a marriage, and I cannot stress enough to beware of *Outside Forces* when you are working toward *Defending the Integrity of your Union*.

6.1 Group Session

"Give honor to marriage, and remain faithful to one another in marriage. God will surely judge people who are immoral and those who commit adultery."
Hebrews 13:4 NLT

Hopefully, you paid close attention and took to heart the materials from chapters three, four, and five, because these next two chapters, especially this one, have the potential to stir up some heated emotions or resentment. We ask that you be open and honest in your discussions with your spouse, as well as gentle and kind in your responses. Let's take a look at what John 3:20-21 has to say about tough situations like this:

"Everyone who does evil hates the light, and will not come into the light for fear that their deeds will be exposed. But whoever lives by the truth comes into the light, so that it may be seen plainly that what they have done has been done in the sight of God."

Please keep in mind that we are not saying that anyone has sinned by not discussing the concerns in this chapter, but it goes along with the idea that everything must first be brought to light before positive change or healing can begin.

When I joined the U.S. Air Force in 1991, I took an oath to defend my country against all enemies foreign and domestic. While serving my country was very important to me, it will never compare to serving my God and protecting my family. My primary responsibility is to my Father, God, then to my wife, and then to my family. Defending the integrity of my marriage not only serves God, my wife, and my family, but it also preserves my own integrity as a man. Like my military oath, my Christian oath signifies that I have a responsibility to defend my God and my marriage against all enemies foreign and domestic – outside forces and inside relationships. Through this ministry, I have made a solemn commitment to defend God's design for marriage.

Let's jump right in and discuss how outside friendships can impact our marriages. For this group session, let's take a few minutes for each of the couples to go through this section together, then regroup and share some insights.

1. In what specific ways do your friends positively or negatively impact your relationship with your spouse?

2. Do you agree with your partner? What would you add to your spouse's answer?

3. Regarding the negative aspects, what do you feel can be done to turn things around?

4. How do each of you feel about friends of the opposite sex?

5. Are there any friends you are starting to realize you may need to distance yourself from after this discussion?

Go back to the group and discuss some of the conclusions you reached through this discussion.

Types of Friends

There are a few different categories friends can fall into:

- Individual friends or mutual friends

- Existing friends from before your marriage, or new friends you've made during your marriage

- Acquaintances or colleagues

- Couple friends or single friends

Advice on how to handle friends of the opposite sex:

- Respect your spouse's feelings.

- Talk it out: give your spouse a chance to talk about his/her feelings.

- Reassure your spouse about your commitment to your marriage.

- Be diligent about building your spouse's confidence.

- Your spouse's needs and your commitment to your marriage are priority.

- Involve your spouse in your friendships or build them into couple friendships.

- Set boundaries that help your spouse feel more secure and lessen any anxiety that your spouse may be feeling.

- Protective boundaries will let your spouse know that you cherish your relationship and care enough to protect it at all cost.

Some of these concepts may seem irrelevant to you because you're already in a trusting relationship with no fear of infidelity. If that is true, count yourself blessed. Go back and read through the list and try to think of any other area of your life where these points may apply. Share your thoughts with the group.

We caution against the use of individual Bible verses to make a point because there is a danger of them being taken out of context, but we believe the following examples can safely be presented in this manner because they relate consistently with the nature of our enemy, the devil:

Be sober-minded and alert. Your adversary the devil prowls around like a roaring lion, seeking someone to devour. - 1 Peter 5:8

Do not give the devil a foothold. – Ephesians 4:27

From Scott: The reason I used those excerpts of Scripture is that these outside forces we are discussing in this chapter can be used by the devil to undermine our marriages. Unfortunately, I speak from experience when I say that an honest friendship can subtly derail a marriage. In my case, I had such a strong intellectual connection with a female friend that the devil was able to gain a foothold and gradually make me question every other aspect of my marriage. Although there was never a physical or emotional connection, I had still abandoned my post, and the devil quickly devoured that marriage.

Friends are not the only outside force that can drive a wedge between spouses; here is a list of some other sources of strain on our marriages.

1. Work

2. Hobbies

3. Electronics

4. Neighbors

5. Education

6. Finances (We have a later chapter devoted to this.)

7. Politics (Wait! Should this go under conflict?)

8. Addictions

Are there any other items (aside from family, which we will discuss in the next chapter) that you can think of that did not make this list?

Let's take a moment to discuss how these outside sources affect our marriages and how we can effectively deal with them. Feel free to share your personal experiences if you are comfortable doing so.

Letting these outside forces get out of control can result in collateral damage that goes beyond the marriage. In other words, if we let outside forces tear at our marriages, how will this affect other areas of our lives?

6.2 On Your Own

"Give honor to marriage, and remain faithful to one another in marriage. God will surely judge people who are immoral and those who commit adultery."
Hebrews 13:4 NLT

Several years ago when I first started gardening, the parable of the sower became much more meaningful to me.

 Read through the parable in Luke 8:5-8 so it is fresh in your mind.

I have known this parable since I was young, but when I started working the soil with my own hands, the story came to life. When I decided to plant a vegetable garden, my kids were not in school yet, so we spent a lot of time playing in our huge backyard. There was no garden there, so to get one started, I had to dig out the grass in an area, pull out rocks, add in fresh, healthy soil, and plant the vegetables. I can put that all in one sentence as if it was quick and easy, but it was back-breaking work. It took days and days of working for hours and hours. As I worked, the parable of the sower came to mind over and over. Here are some observations I made.

- Good soil does not just happen on its own.

- Even when you think you got all the rocks out, you will still find more.

- Good soil is not immune to weeds.

- When weeds are new and small, they are easy to get rid of.

- When weeds are left to grow, they dig in deeply and are harder to remove.

- Deeply rooted weeds may leave behind an imperceptible root and grow back after you think they're gone.

- Good soil eventually becomes depleted of nutrients and has to be enriched to stay good.

- Threats to your garden's health come from all directions: not just weeds and rocks, but also birds, bugs, extreme heat and other weather events, and disease.

It was a great learning opportunity that I didn't expect when I decided to plant a garden, and you're a pretty smart reader, so you can probably see where I'm going with this. Let's consider how these concepts apply to your marriage.

Take a look back at the bulleted list of advice on how to handle friends of the opposite sex from 6.1. What points listed there do you think could be applied to the wisdom I learned from gardening?

Pray for your marriage.

6.3 Couple Time

"Give honor to marriage, and remain faithful to one another in marriage. God will surely judge people who are immoral and those who commit adultery."
Hebrews 13:4 NLT

Focus on the Heart

One thing we know about Jesus Christ is that he had a strong focus on the *heart* of people. And your marriage maintenance depends on the heart, too.

Read Matthew 5:27-30 together.

From Carla: It's pretty harsh sounding, right? Here's the thing. I had a close friend who was male, and there was something about him that made my husband uncomfortable. It caused anxiety and strain, so I had to consider what it says in verse 29. "It is better for you to lose one part of your body than for your whole body to be thrown into hell." The thought of going to hell because of a friendship seems extreme, I know. But look at what it says in verse 28. Write down what Jesus says is the equivalent to adultery.

For both examples, the eye and the hand, the only reason given to get rid of them is that they cause you to stumble. And those sentences are the ones immediately after the command not to commit adultery, so the natural conclusion to me is that anything that is a threat, or even feels like a threat, needs to be cut off and thrown away. Do you have any friendships that need to be cut off? It isn't easy, but your marriage will be better off in the long run.

Take time to pray together and ask God to bless this work you're doing and to bless your marriage. You may come up with your own prayer and speak from the heart, or if you can't think of what to say, you can say this prayer:

> Loving Lord,
> There are so many challenges to the integrity of our union in this world today. Please give us discernment as we encounter these external influences on our marriage. Please help us to improve essential relationships that are negatively impacting our union, give us the foresight to avoid situations that may cause undue strain upon our marriage, and give us the fortitude to eliminate unhealthy relationships and vices that are damaging our lives and our relationship. Father, we thank You for equipping us with the ability to fend off attacks and preserve the integrity of our marriage. Lord, we thank You for being there for us: protecting us, guiding us, and strengthening us to maintain the marriage that You designed for us.
> In Jesus' name, Amen.

Here's a place to write your own prayer if you want to keep a record of it. At the end of this program, look back on the prayers you've written and see what God has done over these 10 weeks.

Action Plan:

Take a good look at the relationships you have outside your marriage. Do any of them need to be addressed with your spouse?

Be intentional about protecting your marriage.

If there is anything you feel you need to keep from your spouse, think hard about it. Remember, every-thing needs to be done in the light, not in the dark, hidden spaces. Be open with your spouse so you can protect your marriage together.

Don't only focus on the things to get rid of, but also nourish your marriage with the things it needs to flourish.

Chapter 7

DEFENDING THE INTEGRITY OF YOUR UNION: FAMILY

7.0 Preparing Your Heart

"If it is possible, as far as it depends on you, live at peace with everyone." Romans 12:18

Objective: This week we will plan and implement ways to defend and protect the unity of our marriage from potential threats or issues stemming from within the family.

From Scott:

In the book of Ruth, a widowed woman named Naomi was left with her two daughters-in-law after her sons passed. The two Moabite women, Ruth and Orpah, set off with their mother-in-law to return to her land of Judah. When Naomi released them to return to their own land, Ruth declined, saying: "Where you go I will go, and where you stay I will stay. Your people will be my people and your God my God. Where you die I will die, and there I will be buried" (Ruth 1:16-17).

Ruth committed to remaining with her mother-in-law until the day she died, putting the needs of her mother-in-law over her own. In return, Naomi helped Ruth find a husband to take care of her. His name was Boaz, and he was a relative of her late husband. Finally, Ruth bore an heir for Naomi, a son, named Obed. Through Obed flowed the lineage of our Savior, Jesus (Ruth 3:1, Ruth 4:13-17).

I would say there is a slim chance many of us would make the same kind of commitment to our in-laws as Ruth made to hers. Paul instructed us, in Romans 12:18, to do all that we can to live at peace with everyone, and *everyone* includes our in-laws. However, we must do all that we can to first honor our spouses, and that may entail defending the integrity of our marriages in any conflict with our own families.

7.1 Group Session

"If it is possible, as far as it depends on you, live at peace with everyone." Romans 12:18

Let's take a few minutes for each of the couples to go through this section together, then regroup and share some insights, like we did last week.

1. In what specific ways does your family positively or negatively impact your relationship with your spouse?

2. Do you agree with your partner on that last question? What would you add to your spouse's answer?

3. Regarding the negative aspects, what do you feel can happen to change this?

Did you notice, from chapter 6, the U.S. Air Force oath included defending our country against domestic threats? Those threats from within are like the threats that may exist within our families.

Remember my story about gardening in chapter 6? That same year, when I was playing in the backyard with the kids, I noticed a vine growing up along my fence. It was well established by the time I saw it, and it was poison ivy. I immediately thought, 'There's a lesson here.' Things can creep in unnoticed and take root. Poisonous things. Dangerous things. And they are not easy to get rid of, but the work is worth it in order to protect your family.

Read 1 Thessalonians 5:20-22 and fill in the missing information here: "Do not treat prophecies with contempt but _____ them all; hold on to what is _____, reject _____ _____ of evil."

A sermon can be a prophecy, and so can an intuition or a simple thought or observation, like the ones that came to me as I was gardening. But not all prophecies (or thoughts or sermons or intuitions) are from God, which is why you need to "test them all," as the Apostle Paul wrote in 1 Thessalonians.

You may see the word "prophecy" and think we're starting to talk about psychics and fortune-tellers, but that is not the purpose of that word in the Bible. A prophecy is a message from God.

One way to test messages to see whether they are from God is to compare them to the nature we know of Jesus. You've probably heard stories of people who said, "God told me to kill these people," or something like that. That is an extreme example and it is obviously not the nature of God. One way I test the prodding I believe is from God is by comparing it to my own nature. If it goes against my nature AND aligns with the nature of God, then it is almost certainly from God.

Here's an example: When God told Scott to write this book and start this ministry, Scott's immediate reaction was to think, 'Who am I to do this? I'm a failure at marriage." It took several messages from several different people and places to finally get through to Scott that this was really God's plan.

Then, when God told Scott to approach people and tell them about it, it was also counterintuitive. Scott is an introvert and feels awkward approaching people to talk. He especially doesn't like to talk to groups or teach. So clearly, this was from God. It follows God's nature and it doesn't follow Scott's. And might I add, when Scott talks to people about this ministry he is inspired. He is eloquent like no other time because he is following the leading of God.

Have you experienced a time when you "heard" God speak to you? I put the word *heard* in quotes because most people I know do not hear God's voice in their ears. Most people would describe it more like a feeling or sense. Talk about those experiences with the group.

Family Relationships: Connectedness and Flexibility

In 2021, Drs. Les & Leslie Parrott wrote a book entitled *Helping Couples*.[17] This section is based on information in their chapter entitled *Family Ties Pull Strings*.

The Parrotts discuss three levels of connection and three levels of flexibility in families. These characteristics are applicable to the marriage, to the immediate family (husband, wife, and children), and to other familial relationships (parents, siblings, etc.).

Family Connectedness:

1. **Disconnected** families are often emotionally detached and have little involvement with one another. These relationships may carry an

abundance of secrets, lack a sense of loyalty, and display feelings of indifference.

2. Families that are **overly connected** may lack individuality and be held together by dependence on one another. Loyalty is demanded, and relationships are focused inward with minimal outside friendships and interests.

3. Families with a **balanced** connection maintain a reasonable level of interaction, share a healthy emotional bond, and experience freedom from interdependence.

Family Flexibility:

1. **Inflexible** families are marked by stringent rules that control every aspect of their lives. Everything is in its place, but family members often feel fearful, resulting in somber moods and a lack of self-expression.

2. **Overly flexible** families are often disorganized, lack leadership, have no set rules or boundaries, and individual needs are seldom met; chaos and dysfunction ensue.

3. Families with **balanced** flexibility easily adjust and adapt to ever-changing situations, fulfilling their present needs. This supportive family unit fosters confidence, stability, and trust.

Each of the categories discussed above includes the two polar extremes and a balanced state. Chances are that your family falls somewhere between these extremes. There is no magic formula for balance, as all families have a different set of personalities, and we need to figure out the right mix.

Take a moment to rate your relationships based on connectedness and flexibility as discussed above:

Your marriage:

Disconnected	Somewhat Disconnected	Balanced	Very Connected	Overly Connected
Inflexible	Somewhat Inflexible	Balanced	Very Flexible	Overly Flexible

Your immediate family:

Disconnected	Somewhat Disconnected	Balanced	Very Connected	Overly Connected
Inflexible	Somewhat Inflexible	Balanced	Very Flexible	Overly Flexible

Your In-laws:

Disconnected	Somewhat Disconnected	Balanced	Very Connected	Overly Connected
Inflexible	Somewhat Inflexible	Balanced	Very Flexible	Overly Flexible

Feel free to share your personal experiences or some examples of each of these relationships.

How do you feel families can move from each extreme toward more of a balance?

7.2 On Your Own

"If it is possible, as far as it depends on you, live at peace with everyone." Romans 12:18

How can we enrich and fertilize the soil?

Here are a few recommendations directly from the Scriptures.

 Galatians 6:9-10a "Let us not become weary in doing good, for at the proper time we will reap a harvest if we do not give up. Therefore, as we have opportunity, let us do good to all people..."

Write your paraphrase of that verse.

What is something good that you do that doesn't get the acknowledgment you think it should get?

How does your perseverance in doing that good thing bless your home or your marriage?

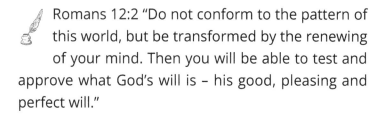 Romans 12:2 "Do not conform to the pattern of this world, but be transformed by the renewing of your mind. Then you will be able to test and approve what God's will is – his good, pleasing and perfect will."

How do we become transformed?

What are some ways you can transform your mindset into one that will make a positive change in your marriage?

Pray for your marriage.

7.3 Couple Time

"If it is possible, as far as it depends on you, live at peace with everyone." Romans 12:18

Let's continue to look at some Scripture together.

Ephesians 4:26-27(NLT) "And 'don't sin by let- ting anger control you.' Don't let the sun go down while you are still angry, for anger gives a foothold to the devil."

What can control you and give the devil a way into your relationship?

Continuing shortly after that last verse it says, "Don't use foul or abusive language. Let every- thing you say be good and helpful so that your words will be an encouragement to those who hear them." Ephesians 4:29 NLT

What should your words do?

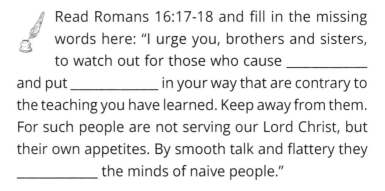

Read Romans 16:17-18 and fill in the missing words here: "I urge you, brothers and sisters, to watch out for those who cause _____ and put _____ in your way that are contrary to the teaching you have learned. Keep away from them. For such people are not serving our Lord Christ, but their own appetites. By smooth talk and flattery they _____ the minds of naive people."

Ephesians 4:2-3 (NLT) says, "Always be humble and gentle. Be patient with each other, making allowance for each other's faults because of your love. Make every effort to keep yourselves united in the Spirit, binding yourselves together with peace."

What are we to do with each other's faults and why?

How much effort are we supposed to put into keeping ourselves united?

One final thought: "Be alert and of sober mind. Your enemy the devil prowls around like a roaring lion looking for someone to devour." 1 Peter 5:8

Take time to pray together and ask God to bless this work you're doing and to bless your marriage. You may come up with your own prayer

and speak from the heart, or if you can't think of what to say, you can say this prayer:

> Father God,
> Scripture teaches us that when we marry, we become as one flesh. Additionally, what was two families has now become as one family. Lord, in honoring our spouses we should offer patience to our in-laws. Please give us the fortitude to speak with respect to them and about them as we strive to live in peace and unity as You have called us to do. As we are of one flesh, help us defend our spouses and our marriages, should our family come against them. Finally, Father, we ask that You work in our hearts, as well as theirs, to develop an understanding that draws us closer in love and brings glory to You.
> In Jesus' name, Amen.

Use this space to write your own prayer — and there's more space on the back of this page — if you want to keep a record of it. At the end of this program, look back on the prayers you've written and see what God has done over these 10 weeks.

Action Plan:

Be watchful for negative impacts on your marriage from within your family. Work together with your spouse to find ways to confront the situation or make a positive change.

Keep doing the good you know you should be doing.

Find ways to renew your mind and transform your mindset in positive ways.

Be encouraging. Keep the peace.

Pay attention to prodding from the Lord.

Chapter 8

FINANCIAL FAITHFULNESS

8.0 Preparing Your Heart

"And God is able to bless you abundantly, so that in all things at all times, having all that you need, you will abound in every good work." 2 Corinthians 9:8

Objective: This week we will create a plan for managing finances and avoiding conflicts that may come from financial stress.

From Scott:

I remember learning early in life that we needed to give 10% back to God, and the church called it a **tithe**. The Old Testament says that "a tithe of everything from the land ... belongs to the Lord" (Leviticus 27:30). In fact, the Hebrew word for tithe, *ma'aser (ma-uh-SARE)*, literally means "a tenth." In the New Testament, Paul encouraged Christians to give generously, consistently, and joyfully: "everyone gave as they were able and even beyond their ability" (2 Corinthians 8:3), "on the first day of the week, everyone should set aside a sum of money" (1 Corinthians 16:2), "each of you should give what you have decided in your heart to give, not reluctantly or under compulsion" (2 Corinthians 9:7).

As I grew up I only gave because I had to. I did not give generously, I did not give consistently, and I certainly did not give joyfully. I eventually learned that I was not giving with the attitude that the Lord asked of me and I started working toward giving consistently, then joyfully, then generously. Speaking of giving generously, have you heard Robert Gilmour LeTourneau? If not, you may have heard about LeTourneau University, the institution in Longview, Texas, that he and his wife, Evelyn, founded. RG LeTourneau was a Christian businessman known for contributing 90% of his business and personal income to Christian causes around the world.[18] Granted, this man was quite wealthy, but how many wealthy people give away 90% of their income while they are living? Is it reasonable to believe their wealth was a blessing from God in response to their faithfulness and generosity? See Malachi 3:10.

8.1 Group Session

"And God is able to bless you abundantly,
so that in all things at all times,
having all that you need, you will abound
in every good work." 2 Corinthians 9:8

"Money cannot buy happiness" is an expression that has been around for a long time. Unfortunately, no matter how many times people hear that phrase, they still think that they can prove it wrong. The fact is that when they buy something to make them happy, they always need more; the house is not big enough, the car is not fancy enough, the boat is not fast enough, or the bling is not … "blingy" enough. What if someone suggested that this pursuit of money and things is not about more money and more things, but about missing a closeness to God?

Read Matthew 6:19-24.

- Why is it futile to try to accumulate wealth here on earth?

- In verse 21, Matthew writes, "for where your treasure is, there your heart will be also." What does that mean?

- Can you have money and "earthly" treasures

and still serve God?

Of course you can! God is not asking us to live in abject poverty. As you continue in this chapter, you will see the ways God uses the money entrusted to us in ways that serve others.

Take a minute to reflect upon what heaven may be like. How does this compare with what happiness is on earth?

The Bible reminds us that "He will wipe every tear from their eyes. There will be no more death or mourning or crying or pain" (Revelation 21:4) and that "'What no eye has seen, what no ear has heard, and what no human mind has conceived' - the things God has prepared for those who love Him" (1 Corinthians 2:9). Whatever you thought about in that brief reflection ... God has something even more amazing in store for us. Now that really speaks of happiness!

Before Carla and I got married, we worked together through the book *Preparing for Marriage: Discover God's Plan for a Lifetime of Love*.[19] There is one chapter that talks about money, and the following statements are some important points that we gleaned from that chapter. Listen as the facilitators read these points, then fill in the blanks with the missing words.

- It is not a lack of money that causes the biggest problems in a marriage, but our _____ toward it and our _____ about it.

- How we handle money reveals something about our _____, _____, _____, and _____ with God.

- Handling our finances is the biggest test of _____ in our marriages.

- Because we are _____ of God's resources, all of our _____ decisions are actually _____ decisions.

- The resources that God entrusts us with are used to accomplish His _____ and _____.

Materialism vs. Financial Faithfulness

Materialism is one of Satan's most effective tactics in trying to distract us from figuring out what we need to make us truly happy. We combat our sinful desire for materialism through **financial faithfulness**.

Here are some principles John Moore and Associates[20] say are key to financial faithfulness. How do you define the following principles of financial faithfulness?

Accountability

Stewardship

Generosity

Transparency

Loyalty

Community

How can materialism damage our marriages?

How can financial faithfulness help our marriages?

 ## Keys to Financial Wellness[21]

1. Spend less than you make (Luke 12:15) – Be on your guard against _____.

2. Be prudent about debt (Romans 13:8) – Clearly from this Scripture it is not wrong to have temporary debt, just do not let it remain outstanding. What is one idea that will help to ensure a debt does not remain outstanding?

3. Build Liquidity (Proverbs 21:5) – Profit is the result of the plans of _____ people.

4. Set long-term goals (Isaiah 32:8) - A synonym of "noble" is "honorable." Read that scripture again and use the word "honorable" in place of "noble."

5. Act like a manager, not an owner (1 Corinthians 10:26) – Who actually owns the earth and everything in it? _____ How would it change the way you use your possessions (car, house, money, etc), if you considered yourself a manager rather than an owner?

6. Give generously (2 Corinthians 9:7) – What should be our attitude as we give generously?

Is there a stipulation that we only need to be generous if we live above poverty level?

The Path to Financial Intimacy[22]

Jot down one example of what each of these 10 actions would look like in your marriage at this stage of your lives.

1. Include God.

2. Become financial partners.

3. Define specific shared goals.

4. Combine financial resources.

5. Share financial responsibilities.

6. Develop the budget together and meet regularly.

7. Remove financial pressures or take steps to alleviate them.

8. Agree on monetary guidelines.

9. Consult with a financial professional.

10. Place the needs of the family above individual desires.

8.2 On Your Own

"And God is able to bless you abundantly, so that in all things at all times, having all that you need, you will abound in every good work." 2 Corinthians 9:8

Reflect on the following Scriptures. Use the space below each scripture to journal about thoughts that come to your mind.

I Timothy 6:17-19: "Command those who are rich in this present world not to be arrogant nor to put their hope in wealth, which is so uncertain, but to put their hope in God, who richly provides us with everything for our enjoyment. Command them to do good, to be rich in good deeds, and to be generous and willing to share. In this way they will lay up treasure for themselves as a firm foundation for the coming age, so that they may take hold of the life that is truly life."

Proverbs 11:24-25: "One man gives freely, yet gains even more; another withholds unduly, but comes to poverty. A generous man will prosper; he who refreshes others will himself be refreshed"

Psalm 37:21: "The wicked borrow and do not repay, but the righteous give generously."

Prepare for the couple-time discussion. Go back through the 10 concepts in the Path to Financial Intimacy from the Group Session this week. Which of those do you need to discuss with your spouse this week?

Make a list of material possessions that you own and services that you subscribe to that are important to you. Now think of what life would be like without those. Keep the list handy and discuss it with your spouse during couple time to see how your thoughts compare.

Pray for your marriage.

8.3 Couple Time

"And God is able to bless you abundantly, so that in all things at all times, having all that you need, you will abound in every good work." 2 Corinthians 9:8

One way that couples can keep financial issues from creeping in and damaging their marriage is to consistently consult with one another about financial matters. The following sections may be slightly different based on whether you are married or engaged, and they may be more complex if you are getting remarried. The main concern is to be open and honest and fully discuss these topics.

From section 8.2, which of the 10 concepts did you write down that the two of you need to discuss?

Financial Disclosure

Use the space below this section if you need more space to answer questions or take notes.

For engaged couples:

- What debts and assets are we individually bringing into the marriage?

- What debts and assets will we incur/acquire as

a result of our marriage?

- How will these debts/assets affect us and how will they be managed?

For married couples:

- What debts and assets do we currently have?

- What effect do they have on our marriage?

- How are they being managed?

- What changes can be made to improve?

For all couples:

- Discuss spending habits - Are you a spender or a saver?

- What are your financial fears from the past, present, and future?

- What are your financial goals and priorities?

- What are your plans for the distribution of assets after you are gone? (Read on for clarification)

One time Carla's mom took Carla and Jennifer, Carla's sister, around the house discussing who gets what when she passes. Although it was strange to witness, it made a lot of sense. Let's say you or your spouse have something passed down from generation to generation, and you have multiple children. Do either of you know which child your spouse wants to have that heirloom? What if you had one child that was fond of something you had, and the others never really cared much about it? Does your spouse know? It may feel awkward, but go ahead and discuss the distribution of assets with your spouse (this includes money and life insurance as well). The awkward conversation now will reduce stress substantially in the long run.

The distribution-of-assets discussion is something particularly important in the case of blended families. In the scenario above, Carla and Jennifer are part of a blended family, so it was a matter of which things come from him and which from her, so which would go to his children, and which would go to hers. Like I said — complicated.

As you think about assets and heirlooms and who you think they should go to, make an informal list here:

Financial Roles

Discuss the financial rules, roles, and responsibilities for your marriage. These financial roles should be discussed prior to marriage but it is never too late, and they should be revisited often. These are just a few examples. Are there more?

Assigning Financial Roles[6]

Task	Husband	Wife	Both
Paying the bills			
Balancing the accounts			
Tracking investments			
Tracking expenses			
Setting up the budget			
Making big purchases			

Take time to pray for your marriage and ask God to bless this work you're doing and bless your marriage. You may come up with your own prayer and speak from the heart, or if you can't think of what to say, you can say this prayer:

Gracious Father,
Scripture provides us with so many narratives as to how money can destroy our relationships. Jesus tells us that it is easier for the camel to pass through the eye of a needle than for a rich man to enter the kingdom of heaven. Money often blinds humanity to what is really important. Please remind us, God, that we

are not owners of money, but financial stewards. Lord, we ask for the financial resources to provide what we need in this life, but we also ask for a heart to give generously to Your kingdom and to those in need. We also ask for a united front as a couple, so that we may be like-minded in our financial stewardship. Father, we thank You for the provision of the financial resources to fulfill our needs, and may we ever fulfill the responsibility of financial stewardship in service to You and others.

In Jesus' name, Amen.

Here's a place to write your own prayer if you want to keep a record of it. At the end of this program, look back on the prayers you've written and see what God has done over these 10 weeks.

Action Plan:

Tithe consistently, joyfully, and generously.

Talk with your spouse regularly and openly about finances and budgeting.

Make an effort to align your financial goals and priorities with those of your spouse.

Chapter 9

VIEWS ON PARENTING

9.0 Preparing Your Heart

"Train up a child in the way he should go and even when he is old he will not depart from it." Proverbs 22:6

Objective: This week we will examine our perspectives on parenting and develop a plan for working as a cohesive parenting unit.

From Carla:

Every stage in parenting is different from the others: preparing for a first child, taking care of a newborn, chasing after toddlers, helping schoolchildren through homework, managing teenagers' schedules, supporting college kids who are learning to become independent, and parenting adult children from afar. I know, this is an oversimplification of the role of parents, and some people will tell you the stage you're in is much easier than a later stage. But, let's face it. They're all hard.

One reason they are hard is because every time we reach a new stage, it's something completely foreign to any other stage in our lives. Before my first baby was born, I'd never had my own baby. Before my first-born started school, I'd never had a child in school. You get the picture. And it doesn't help that each child is completely different from each other child. Their needs are different, their personalities are different, and their likes and dislikes are different, so there is no getting-used-to any stage.

If you don't have children yet, don't let this scare you off. Every stage is also full of wonder and beauty and love. But sometimes we don't see the wonder and beauty and love when we're in the thick of it. And every new stage may seem harder than the one before, but that is just because you had just started feeling like you had everything managed before it all changed. But also, every new stage can be more fun than every stage before.

9.1 Group Session

"Train up a child in the way he should go and even when he is old he will not depart from it." Proverbs 22:6

This chapter may be another thing that doesn't seem relevant to you. Maybe you have made the decision not to have children, maybe you have raised your children and are empty-nesters, or maybe you feel like you've figured this part out. If it's the latter, clue us in on your secret! But no matter what situation you're in, this chapter will have some helpful insight and ideas for you on how to relate to people and will give you insight into others' personalities. And most importantly, it will give you a new perspective on our relationship with God, our Father.

Five Parenting Styles:

Read through each of these descriptions and see if any of them resonate with you. Maybe they describe your parenting style or your spouse's, maybe they describe your parents' styles, or maybe they remind you of someone else you are close to.

1. **Balanced -** warm and nurturing, emotionally supportive, responsive, and consistent and fair discipline

2. **Uninvolved -** low emotional connection and responsiveness, high independence of child, and highly negotiable rules loosely enforced

3. **Permissive** - overly protective and very responsive, more of a friend to their child, and lenient with discipline

4. **Strict** - strictly enforced rules, firm discipline, low responsiveness and low emotional connection

5. **Overbearing** - overly protective, caters to every need, a friend to their child, and strictly enforces rules with firm discipline[1]

Parenting Styles and Childhood Experiences:

As a married couple, there should be a discussion on whether you have a desire to have children and when to do so. Hopefully that discussion happened before you got married. The next important discussion relating to children is how to raise them.

1. Discuss some of your memorable childhood experiences.

2. What were your parents' parenting styles? What parenting styles have you adopted or are most likely to adopt if you do not yet have children?

3. What are some important expectations, behaviors, actions, or environments in your relationship with your children that benefit their spiritual training and nurture?

4. Discuss how children affect careers, family roles, intimacy, and the marriage relationship.

God's example of parenting:

God gives us an example on how to parent. He disciplines us and expects us to discipline our children. Read Hebrews 12:7-11.

What is a sign that we are true, legitimate sons and daughters of our parents?

In verse 9, what is the natural response to discipline from our parents?

Of course discipline is hard for parents and children alike. In verse 11 we see confirmation of that, but what is the result of discipline?

The God of the Old Testament:

Some may look at the example set by God, especially some of the Old Testament stories, and envision God as an overbearing parent. It's easy to think that when you read stories like the one in 1 Chronicles 13 when Uzzah was struck dead for touching the ark of God, even though he was just trying to steady it and keep it from falling. That feels very harsh and unyielding. I am inclined to agree.

Can you think of another example of "overbearing" discipline from God in the Old Testament?

Is He the same God in the New Testament?

When we see the love that Jesus, who is God, demonstrates in the New Testament, sometimes it is hard to reconcile that with the God of the Old Testament. What is a particularly loving interaction you can think of between Jesus and someone who was hurting?

 One example is found in Matthew 9:20-22, which is the only recorded time Jesus called someone "daughter." Take a minute to read that story.

What is a time in the New Testament when Jesus corrected, rebuked, or disciplined someone?

There may be multiple stories you can think of when Jesus rebuked someone who opposed him, but one interesting story that comes to mind is about a rebuke directed toward the disciples, and this isn't the only one of its kind. This particular one is found in Luke 9:52-56. Read the passage and then answer these questions:

Jesus and his disciples were traveling through what region?

Do you remember what we learned about the Samaritans and the Jews in Chapter 2 of this book?

What did the disciples want to do in verse 54?

What would be the purpose of that action? Would it lead to repentance? Would it turn the people's hearts toward God? Would it glorify God in any way?

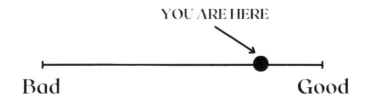

It doesn't work like this!

God's law isn't arbitrary. There is a purpose for every command He gave us, even though we don't always understand His purposes yet. There is an important reason we see a vast difference between the God of the Old Testament and the God of the New Testament. God is holy. He is good. He is perfect. There can be no link between God and anything evil or impure. Not one thing that is evil or imperfect can survive in God's presence. So here's the bad news: we are evil.

I know, we like to think of ourselves as good people, but we are not perfect in any way, shape, or form, which means we are evil. There isn't a continuum, like the one above, that says good on one end and bad on the other end, where we hope to be in the gray area somewhere between mediocre and good. There is only good and not good. There is no gray area in between.

The Old Testament established the law and the consequences of not following the law. The consequences were unwavering. The only way to receive purification from disobedience was through sacrifice, and the sacrifices of the Old Testament were only a temporary fix.

We have to completely understand the cost of evil, disobedience, impurity, imperfection, unholiness, or whatever word you want to use to label sin. We have to firmly grasp the concept of that *cost.* Then we can completely understand the *grace* that is given to us through the sacrifice of Jesus Christ. God cannot tolerate sin. Christ sacrificed Himself for us to give us grace. Christ is God. God wants to have a relationship with us. No one else, past, present or future, would be willing to go to such lengths for that relationship. His sacrifice is what made it possible. There is no difference between the God of the two testaments.

9.2 On Your Own

"Train up a child in the way he should go and even when he is old he will not depart from it." Proverbs 22:6

The group session was intense this week. Take a look back and answer these questions based on the information there:

1. What keeps us from being called "good," as God is called good?

2. Why does God discipline us? HINT: HEBREWS 12:10

3. What connections can you draw from the group session and your parenting style?

Look back at the list of parenting styles in the group session of this chapter. Which of the styles have you witnessed going wrong?

Be honest with yourself about which style matches you. Write it here.

What characteristics of that style are you pleased with?

What characteristics are you displeased with?

Which one matches your spouse's parenting style?

What characteristics of that style are you pleased with?

What characteristics are you displeased with?

 Pray for your marriage.

9.3 Couple Time

"Train up a child in the way he should go and even when he is old he will not depart from it." Proverbs 22:6

Family Planning:

(If you're already parents, feel free to skip these four questions) If you have not yet begun your family, there are some important things to discuss prior to marriage. The marriage will certainly suffer serious setbacks if expectations regarding children are drastically different. Here are some things to consider and discuss:

1. Do you both want to have children?

2. How many children do you desire to have?

3. How soon do you want children?

4. What is the desired age gap between each child?

Keeping the relationship bonds strong:

Remember the Marriage Commitment Triangle in Chapter 2? When children are thrown in the mix, things become much more complicated. There are bonds stretching here and there, and the number of relationship ties you are concerned with will quickly multiply from the two you originally had, and as a parent, you are also responsible for helping your children develop and maintain their bonds with God.

Take some time to doodle on this image. Add the lines representing your children or future children, your

grandchildren, step-children, and any other relationships that factor in.

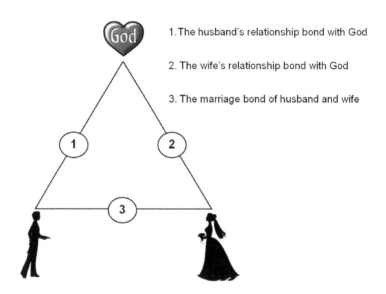

1.The husband's relationship bond with God

2. The wife's relationship bond with God

3. The marriage bond of husband and wife

Does a drawn representation of those relationships
feel overwhelming? If it does, it's not unusual. With
Scott having six kids and me having three kids …
Phew! Add in the lines to connect each of us with
each other's kids and the lines from all of the kids

to God, it is very complicated. Yours may look more simple than this, but that doesn't mean it is simple. Every added line adds challenges. That is the point of this exercise: to recognize the complexity of the added relationships and the importance of keeping all of those bonds strong.

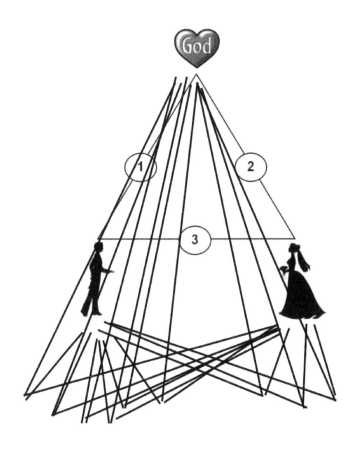

Now and in every situation, we need the help of the Holy Spirit. Lean into God for the strength to keep the structure of your bonds intact. Nurture all of those relationships and pray for them.

Take time to pray together and ask God to bless this work you're doing and to bless your marriage. You may come up with your own prayer and speak from the heart, or if you can't think of what to say, you can say this prayer:

> Father,
> You are the model of a perfect parent, and You call us to raise up our children to know and to serve You. Lord, we thank You for the patience, grace, mercy, and love that You show us as your children. Unfortunately, our sin tries to lead us in a direction to shirk our responsibilities as parents. Father God, please keep us fully alert to our responsibilities to our children. Encourage us to reflect Your love upon them, let Your Spirit speak through us as we teach them about You, grant us patience as we help them learn to navigate life, and strengthen us in grace and mercy to pick them up when they fall. Father, lead us, for we cannot do this alone, but only with Your counsel and instruction.
> In Jesus' name, Amen.

Here's a place to write your own prayer if you want to keep a record of it. At the end of this program, look back on the prayers you've written and see what God has done over these 10 weeks.

Action Plan:

Pray for your children.

Teach your children discipline.

Keep an intentional focus on the positive aspects of your parenting style.

Pray for God's help in improving the aspects of your parenting style that you are displeased with.

Chapter 10

LOVE, AFFECTION, AND INTIMACY

10.0 Preparing Your Heart

"However, each of you also must love his wife as he loves himself, and the wife must respect her husband." Ephesians 5:33

Objective: This week we will identify and commit to ways to achieve, improve, and maintain a deep level of intimacy in our marriages.

From Scott:

Do you know the song *Love and Marriage*? In it, Frank Sinatra repeatedly crooned the lyrics "love and marriage go together like a horse and carriage," and "you can't have one without the other." Technically, that is not true. Can you love someone and not be married?

Can you be married without love? The answer to both of those questions is *yes*. Now, can you have a horse without a carriage or a carriage and no horse? Of course!

Have you heard the phrase: you're putting the cart before the horse? The horse can probably *push* the carriage, but it is much more efficient for the horse to *pull* the carriage. If you have no horse, though, the carriage is pretty useless, right? I believe the same analogy can be applied to love and marriage.

If I only have love, things are still pretty good. After all, Jesus gave us a commandment to love one another as He loves us (John 13:34 ESV). If I am married to someone whom I do not love, things are not going to go well.

There is a common theme in the first part of 1 Corinthians 13; no matter what positive actions I carry out, without love I am nothing, and I have gained nothing (1 Corinthians 13:2-3, NIV). In preparation for this session, reflect upon the love you share with your spouse.

10.1 Group Session

"However, each of you also must love his wife as he loves himself, and the wife must respect her husband." Ephesians 5:33

What is Intimacy?

- Intimacy doesn't just mean sex - it is so much more than that.

- Intimacy is the closeness in a relationship that allows each person to share and uncover private thoughts, emotions, experiences, dreams, and insecurities.

- Intimacy motivates each person in a relationship to trust one another and make sacrifices for each other.

- Intimacy is the ability for each person to feel what the other is feeling and understand one another's needs.[1]

Let's dive deeper into that bulleted list you just read.

What are some of the benefits of closeness in a relationship?

Complete this sentence *(The answers are in the bulleted list)*: Intimacy _____ each person to trust one another and _____ _____ for each other.

How does intimacy impact the empathy couples feel for each other?

Types of Intimacy: Listen as the facilitator explains the different types of intimacy and jot down a glimpse of what each of these means[26].

Spiritual -

Recreational -

Intellectual -

Physical -

Emotional -

_____ intimacy is the foundational bond from which other forms of intimacy grow.

Recreational intimacy is also referred to as _____ intimacy.

_____ intimacy is typically highest near the _____ of the relationship. As the relationship progresses, the _____ increases and the exploration of one another's worlds diminishes.

Males typically feel most connected when _____ intimacy is highest.

Females typically feel most connected when _____ intimacy is highest.

Take a few minutes with the group to discuss specific activities in each category that can contribute to growth in these types of intimacy.

Spiritual -

Recreational -

Intellectual -

Physical -

Emotional -

Love vs Affection

Affection leads to contentment and safety, intimacy and closeness, satisfaction and feeling cared for, and anticipation.

LOVE is the foundation of a successful marriage, but AFFECTION takes love to a "deeper realm of tender expression."[27]

Love...	Affection...
Is patient	Is empathetic
Is kind	Is tender
Is never rude	Thoughtfully apologizes
Is not self-seeking	Comforts a discouraged spouse
Does not delight in evil	Carefully uncovers sin and offers grace
Never fails	Binds and confirms unfailing love

[17] Randy Carlson, *Starved for Affection* (Carol Stream: Tyndale House Publishers, Inc., 2005), 66

Remember the list we asked you to write at the end of chapter one, section two? It was a list of things you can pray for your spouse. Flip back to that page now and refresh your memory.

Marriage should be a safe zone where both partners feel freedom to express needs and insecurities without fear of humiliation or judgement. Even if it is safe, though, people often fear showing what they view as a weakness or failure on their own part.

*Since this is a group session, there may be some embarrassment reading this next part aloud, so everyone just read the next **two** paragraphs silently:*

To husbands: Often, women are embarrassed because they feel their bodies respond too slowly to sexual stimulation, and a climax takes too long. So, many women will "fake it" because they are afraid you will get bored or annoyed with them. Your job is to reassure your wife that you want her to feel that pleasure and that her pleasure brings you pleasure.

To wives: Sometimes, men are insecure because they "finish" before you do, so they feel bad about not giving you the time you need, but at the same time, they don't want to tell you that, because it may feel to him like an admission of weakness. Or sometimes they are insecure because body and hormone changes make it harder for them to get an erection. Either way, wives, it is your job to support your husband. It will be hard for him to believe he can still make you happy, but you can give him that reassurance. And the next time it happens, he'll need that reassurance, again.

To both: Sometimes there is the issue of past trauma: One spouse doesn't want to trigger the survivor of that trauma, or the survivor feels triggered without their spouse knowing it.

In all of the situations we just read, feelings of inadequacy are the issue and communication is the answer. It is okay to feel vulnerable with your spouse. Vulnerability is part of intimacy.

Now back to that list of things to pray about from 1.2:

Notice affection is on the list? You can also pray for your own physiological response to that affection. God created our bodies and the way they respond to stimulation. Why would we think He doesn't care if we are sexually aroused or satisfied by our spouses? He created us to feel that arousal and pleasure. It isn't something we figured out on our own. It isn't a surprise to God or something to keep hidden from Him. It's a gift from Him! Sometimes the stress of life or our health issues disrupt that sexual pleasure, but God is able to reignite the fire, so pray for it.

10.2 On Your Own

"However, each of you also must love his wife as he loves himself, and the wife must respect her husband." Ephesians 5:33

Types of Intimacy

What suggestions from the group discussion are you willing to add to your interactions with your spouse in order to enhance your intimacy?

Spiritual -

Recreational -

Intellectual -

Physical -

Emotional -

Which of these are weakest between you?

Which are strongest?

Which would you like to see grow more?

Which do you think your partner would like to see grow more?

What can you do to make that happen?

The 5 Love Languages[28]: The ways we express and experience love

1. Words of affirmation - spoken praise and appreciation for your spouse

2. Quality time - offering your spouse undivided attention for a period of time, whether in activity or conversation.

3. Receiving gifts - giving your spouse a thoughtful gift.

4. Acts of service - carrying out a special act in service to your spouse

5. Physical touch - this simple act of touching your spouse can make them feel loved

Do you know each other's love languages? Everyone usually has two: a primary and a secondary.

What are yours?

What do you think are your spouse's?

 Take a look at I Peter 4:8 write the verse here.

What tangible ways can you show your love in your spouse's love languages this week?

 Pray for your marriage. Then go on to the next page.

Remember that list of things to pray for from chapter one? What answers have you seen over these past 10 weeks?

10.3 Couple Time

"However, each of you also must love his wife as he loves himself, and the wife must respect her husband." Ephesians 5:33

Compare answers on what love languages you have. Did you guess your spouse's love languages right?

It is important to communicate your love languages to your spouse because our tendency is to show our love in a manner that matches our *own* love languages, and that may not be satisfying to our partners at all.

Now this may be a little awkward, but did you realize the Bible actually has commands regarding a married couple's sex life? Actually, the Apostle Paul calls it a

concession rather than a command, but it is important enough advice to be written in the Bible. Look up
I Corinthians 7:5 and fill in the blanks below.

"Do not _____ each other except perhaps by _____
_____ and for __ _____, so that you may devote
yourselves to prayer. Then ____ _____ again so
that Satan will not _____ you because of your lack of
____-_____." I Corinthians 7:5

What was that? You actually are supposed to "come
together" regularly? And why is that?

Fulfilling each other's needs is worth the time and
effort. Take some time to discuss these questions
with your partner:

- How will you balance your time for individual
  pursuits with time for your spouse?

- How likely are you to be able to discuss sensitive issues with your spouse?

- How do you show love and affection for your
  spouse? How will you in the future?

- Will you be able to freely discuss private needs
  and desires with your spouse?

- Do you feel that you understand your partner's feelings?

Take time to pray together and ask God to bless this work you're doing and to bless your marriage. You may come up with your own prayer and speak from the heart, or if you can't think of what to say, you can say this prayer:

> Precious Creator,
> We thank You for accompanying us on this eight-week educational journey and we pray that You will continue to guide us in our marriage going forward. We thank You for the gift of love and intimacy in our marriage. Father, please help us to remain committed to You as well as to each other in this marriage. Instruct us in our communication, guide us through conflict, and help us to defend our faith and the sanctity of our marriage. Please give us the wisdom to be good stewards of the resources You entrust to us. Lord, please lead us in being great parents that search for discernment in all of our familial decisions. Finally, Father God, we thank You for working in us and creating a beacon of light to illuminate Your design for marriage to others.
> In Jesus' name, Amen.

Here's a place to write your own prayer if you want to keep a record of it. Now that we are at the end of this program, look back on the prayers you've written and see what God has done over these 10 weeks. In a year or so, pick this back up and read through them again.

Action Plan:

Find out what areas of intimacy are most important to your spouse.

All five areas of intimacy are important to a healthy marriage. Make sure that none of them are being neglected in your marriage.

Be intentional in addressing all areas of intimacy in your marriage.

Allow yourself to be vulnerable about your insecurities.

1. Geiger, A.W., & Livingston, G. (2019). *8 facts about love and marriage in America.* Pew Research Center. Accessed August 8, 2020 from https://www.pewresearch.org/fact-tank/2 019/02/13/8-facts-about-love-and-marriage/
2. Ripley J. S. & Worthington, E. L. (2014). *Couple therapy: A new hope-focused approach.* Inter-Varsity Press.
3. Ammirati, T. A. (2022). *When is it a good time to seek counseling?* The Gottman Institute web-site. https://www.gottman.com/blog/when-is-it-a-good-time-to-seek-counseling/
4. Gottman, J. (2014). *The 5 types of couples.* The Gottman Institute.
5. Omartian, S. (2014). *The power of a praying wife.* Harvest House Publishers.
6. Rose, S. A., Feldman, J. F., & Jankowski, J. J. (2009). A cognitive approach to the development of early language. *Child Development, 80*(1), 134–150. https://doi.org/10.1111/j.1467-8624.2008.01250.x
7. Collins, J. C., (2001). *Good to great: Why some companies make the leap and others don't.* HarperCollins Publishers.
8. Stupart, Y. (2018). *A guide to premarital counseling.* Paired Life.
9. Lebow, J. L., Chambers, A. L., Christensen, A., & Johnson, S. M. (2012). Research on the treatment of couple distress. *Journal of Marital and Family Therapy, 38*(1), 145–168. https://doi.org/10.1111/j.1752-0606.2011.00249.x

10. Harley, W. F. (2013). *His needs, her needs: Building an affair-proof marriage.* Baker Publishing Group.

11. Ingermanson, R. (2019, May 11). *On the road to Jerusalem with Jesus.* Randy Ingermanson. https://www.ingermanson.com/road-to-jerusalem-with-jesus/

12. Petersen, J. C. (2015) *Why don't we listen better? Communicating & connecting in relationships.* Petersen Publications.

13. Petersen, J. C. (2015). *Why don't we listen better? Communicating & connecting in relationships.* Petersen Publications.

14. Gottman, J. (2014). *The 5 types of couples.* The Gottman Institute.

15. Pondy, L. R. (1967). Organizational conflict: Concepts and models. *Administrative Science Quarterly, 12*(2), 296. https://doi.org/10.2307/2391553

16. Omartian, S. (2014). *The power of a praying wife.* Harvest House Publishers. (Original work published 1997)

17. Parrott, L., Parrott, L., & Olson, D. H. (2021). *Helping couples: Proven strategies for coaches, counselors, & clergy.* Zondervan Books.

18. LeTourneau, R.G. (1972). *Mover of men and mountains: The autobiography of R.G. Letourneau.* Moody Publishers.

19. Boehi, D., Nelson, B., Schulte, J., & Shadrach, L. (2010). *Preparing for marriage: Discover God's plan for a lifetime of love.* (D. Rainey, Ed.). Bethany House Publishers.

20. *Our principles: John Moore Associates.* John Moore Associates. (2022, August 8). Retrieved October 18, 2022, from https://www.johnmoore .com/principles/

21. Moore, J. & Cochran, B. (2022). *6 keys to your financial wellness.* Family Life Radio. https://www.myflr.org/6-keys-to-your-financial-wellness/

22. Ford, C. (2014) *Ten ways to improve financial intimacy in marriage.* Bible Money Matters. Accessed August 15, 2020.

23. Parrott, L. & Parrott, L. (1996). *Questions couples ask.* Zondervan. P 107.

24. Olson, D. H., & Wilde, J. L., (nd). *Five parenting styles based on the Olson Circumplex Model.* Prepare-Enrich. Accessed August 16, 2020

25. Parrott, L., & Parrott L., (1996). *Questions couples ask.* Zondervan. P 94

26. Squires, J., (2019) *5 types of intimacy in a healthy marriage.* Faithit. Accessed August 16, 2020. https://faithit.com/5-types-inimacy-healthy-marriage/

27. Carlson, R. (2005). *Starved for affection.* Tyndale House Publishers, Inc.

28. Chapman, G. D. (2005). *The Five love languages: How to express heartfelt commitment to your mate.* Northfield Publishing.

Answer Key

1.1 GROUP SESSION

MARRIAGE BY THE NUMBERS

- HALF OF ALL AMERICANS OVER THE AGE OF 18 ARE MARRIED.

- THE MEDIAN MARRIAGE AGE FOR MEN IS 30 AND 28 FOR WOMEN.

- FOUR OUT OF EVERY TEN MARRIAGES IS A REMARRIAGE.

- 18 MILLION AMERICANS ARE COHABITATING WITH A PARTNER.

- THE MARRIAGE RATE IN THE US IS 6.8 PER 1000 PEOPLE WHILE THE DIVORCE RATE IS 3.2 PER 1000 PEOPLE.

- 60% OF MARRIAGES ARE FIRST MARRIAGES, 20% HAVE ONE SPOUSE REMARRIED, 20% HAVE BOTH SPOUSES GETTING REMARRIED.

<u>41</u> % OF FIRST MARRIAGES END IN DIVORCE, <u>60</u> % OF SECOND MARRIAGES END IN DIVORCE, AND <u>73</u> % OF THIRD MARRIAGES END IN DIVORCE.

Priority		Reasons for getting married	Percent who gave this reason
Mine	World		
	5	Religious reasons	30%
	2	Lifelong commitment	81%
	7	Legal rights and benefits	23%
	6	Financial stability	28%
	1	Love	88%
	3	Companionship	76%
	4	Children	49%

1.2 ON YOUR OWN

GENESIS 2:24: "THAT IS WHY A MAN <u>LEAVES</u> HIS FATHER AND MOTHER AND <u>IS</u> <u>UNITED</u> TO HIS WIFE, AND THEY BECOME <u>ONE</u> <u>FLESH</u>."

MARK 10:9: "THEREFORE WHAT <u>GOD</u> HAS JOINED TOGETHER, LET NO ONE <u>SEPARATE</u>."

2.1 GROUP SESSION

COUPLES WHO RECEIVE PREMARITAL COUNSELING BEFORE THEIR WEDDING ENJOY A <u>30</u> % HIGHER RATE OF MARITAL SUCCESS.

- <u>44</u> % OF COUPLES AGREE TO PREMARITAL COUNSELING

- <u>75</u> % OF WEDDINGS TAKE PLACE IN SOME TYPE OF RELIGIOUS SETTING

- BETWEEN <u>60</u> % - <u>70</u> % OF MARRIED COUPLES WHO SEEK COUPLES COUNSELING SEE A POSITIVE CHANGE.

- DIVORCE PROCEEDINGS EVERY YEAR INVOLVE MORE THAN

1 MILLION CHILDREN AND INCREASE THE LIKELIHOOD OF THEIR GROWING UP IN POVERTY.

- THE AVERAGE COST OF A WEDDING IS $ 28,000 . PREMARITAL COUNSELING COSTS LESS THAN 1 % OF THIS AMOUNT.

MATTHEW 25:40: "TRULY I TELL YOU, WHATEVER YOU DID FOR ONE OF THE LEAST OF THESE BROTHERS OF MINE, YOU DID FOR ME."

2.3 COUPLE TIME

PROVERBS 11:25: "A GENEROUS PERSON WILL PROSPER; WHOEVER REFRESHES OTHERS WILL BE REFRESHED."

2 CORINTHIANS 9:6 AND 8: IN VERSE 6, WE SEE SOWING SPARINGLY RESULTS IN REAPING SPARINGLY, AND SOWING GENEROUSLY RESULTS IN REAPING GENEROUSLY. VERSE 8: "AND GOD IS ABLE TO BLESS YOU ABUNDANTLY, SO THAT IN ALL THINGS AT ALL TIMES, HAVING ALL THAT YOU NEED, YOU WILL ABOUND IN EVERY GOOD WORK."

4.1 GROUP SESSION

1. PHILIPPIANS 2:14: "DO EVERYTHING WITHOUT GRUMBLING OR ARGUING."

2. EPHESIANS 4:15: "INSTEAD, SPEAKING THE TRUTH IN LOVE, WE WILL GROW TO BECOME IN EVERY RESPECT THE MATURE BODY OF HIM WHO IS THE HEAD, THAT IS, CHRIST."

3. ROMANS 12:17: "DO NOT REPAY ANYONE EVIL FOR EVIL. BE CAREFUL TO DO WHAT IS RIGHT IN THE EYES OF EVERYONE."

7.1 GROUP SESSION

1 THESSALONIANS 5:20-22: "DO NOT TREAT PROPHECIES WITH CONTEMPT BUT TEST THEM ALL; HOLD ON TO WHAT IS GOOD, REJECT EVERY KIND OF EVIL."

7.3 COUPLE TIME

ROMANS 16:17-18: "I URGE YOU, BROTHERS AND SISTERS, TO WATCH OUT FOR THOSE WHO CAUSE <u>DIVISIONS</u> AND PUT <u>OBSTACLES</u> IN YOUR WAY THAT ARE CONTRARY TO THE TEACHING YOU HAVE LEARNED. KEEP AWAY FROM THEM. FOR SUCH PEOPLE ARE NOT SERVING OUR LORD CHRIST, BUT THEIR OWN APPETITES. BY SMOOTH TALK AND FLATTERY THEY <u>DECEIVE</u> THE MINDS OF NAIVE PEOPLE."

8.1 GROUP SESSION

- IT IS NOT THE LACK OF MONEY THAT CAUSES THE BIGGEST PROBLEMS IN A MARRIAGE, BUT OUR <u>ATTITUDE</u> TOWARD IT AND OUR <u>COMMUNICATION</u> ABOUT IT.

- HOW WE HANDLE MONEY REVEALS SOMETHING ABOUT OUR <u>CHARACTER</u>, <u>DESIRES</u>, <u>PRIORITIES</u>, AND <u>RELATIONSHIP</u> WITH GOD.

- HANDLING OUR FINANCES IS THE BIGGEST TEST OF <u>ONE-NESS</u> IN OUR MARRIAGES.

- BECAUSE WE ARE <u>STEWARDS</u> OF GOD'S RESOURCES, ALL OF OUR <u>FINANCIAL</u> DECISIONS ARE ACTUALLY <u>SPIRITUAL</u> DECISIONS.

- THE RESOURCES THAT GOD ENTRUSTS US WITH ARE USED TO ACCOMPLISH HIS <u>PLANS</u> AND <u>PURPOSES</u>.

10.1 GROUP SESSION

SPIRITUAL- THIS IS THE COUPLE'S RELATIONSHIP IN THE WORD, PRAYER, AND WORSHIP.

RECREATIONAL - THIS BOND IS STRENGTHENED THROUGH COUPLES PARTICIPATING IN ACTIVITIES TOGETHER.

INTELLECTUAL - THIS BOND IS STRENGTHENED BY A COUPLE CONNECTING THROUGH ONGOING AND REGULAR DISCUSSIONS.

PHYSICAL - THIS BOND IS CREATED AND NURTURED THROUGH SEXUAL AND NON-SEXUAL PHYSICAL TOUCH.

EMOTIONAL - THIS BOND IS CREATED BY SHARING EXPERIENCES WITH ONE ANOTHER THROUGH EMOTIONS.

INTIMACY MOTIVATES EACH PERSON TO TRUST ONE ANOTHER AND MAKE SACRIFICES FOR EACH OTHER.

SPIRITUAL INTIMACY IS THE FOUNDATIONAL BOND FROM WHICH OTHER FORMS OF INTIMACY GROW.

RECREATIONAL INTIMACY IS ALSO REFERRED TO AS EXPERIENTIAL INTIMACY.

INTELLECTUAL INTIMACY IS TYPICALLY HIGHEST NEAR THE BEGINNING OF THE RELATIONSHIP. AS THE RELATIONSHIP PROGRESSES, THE PRESUMPTIONS INCREASES AND THE EXPLORATION OF ONE ANOTHER'S WORLDS DIMINISHES.

MALES TYPICALLY FEEL MOST CONNECTED WHEN PHYSICAL INTIMACY IS HIGHEST.

FEMALES TYPICALLY FEEL MOST CONNECTED WHEN EMOTIONAL INTIMACY IS HIGHEST.

10.3 COUPLE TIME

I Corinthians 7:5: "DO NOT DEPRIVE EACH OTHER EXCEPT PERHAPS BY MUTUAL CONSENT AND FOR A TIME, SO THAT YOU MAY DEVOTE YOURSELVES TO PRAYER. THEN COME TOGETHER AGAIN SO THAT SATAN WILL NOT TEMPT YOU BECAUSE OF YOUR LACK OF SELF-CONTROL."

About the Authors

Scott M. Cadorette, M.Div., M.B.A.

Scott was born in Adrian, Michigan, and grew up in Rockford, Michigan. He is a veteran of the United States Air Force, where he was stationed in the United Kingdom, Louisiana, and Virginia. He then spent 18 years working for energy and transportation companies in Texas and Oklahoma before moving back to Michigan to work in healthcare. Scott earned a Bachelor of Science from Northwestern Oklahoma State University and a Master of Business Administration from Oklahoma Wesleyan University. He completed a Master of Divinity in Pastoral Counseling from Liberty University in 2021 and is currently pursuing a Doctor of Ministry specializing in Pastoral Counseling at Liberty University.

Carla D. Cadorette, M.Ed.

Carla was born in Dallas, Texas, and grew up as a preacher's kid (PK) in Redlands, California. She is currently an instructor of American Sign Language

(ASL) with over 20 years of teaching experience. Carla earned a Bachelor of Arts in Music and Education from Lubbock Christian University and a Master of Education in Curriculum and Instruction with an emphasis in Instructional Technology from Houston Baptist University. Carla is currently pursuing a Doctor of Education in Curriculum and Instruction from Liberty University.